HEAD, HEART & HANDS

Continuing the Handcrafted Tradition of
the Original Roycroft Artisans

By Joe Kirchmyer

NFB
<<<>>>
Buffalo, NY

ISBN: 978-0692459393

Head, Heart & Hands: Continuing the Handcrafted Tradition of the Original Roycroft Artisans.
1ˢᵗ Edition

1.Roycroft. 2. Handcraft. 3. Elbert Hubbard. 4. Non-Fiction

Special thanks to Maureen Kirchmyer, Lauren Kirchmyer, Andrew Kirchmyer, Deb Muniak, Ron VanOstrand and Scott Webb.

Cover Photograph by Ron VanOstrand

For more information on the Roycrofters-At-Large Association
please visit
www.ralaweb.com

No Frills Buffalo/Amelia Press
<<<>>>
119 Dorchester Road
Buffalo, New York 14213

For more information visit
Nofrillsbuffalo.com

Head, Heart & Hands

Continuing the Handcrafted Tradition of
the Original Roycroft Artisans

<<<>>>

TABLE OF CONTENTS	PAGE

When I was asked by the Roycrofters-At-Large Association a couple of years ago to write profiles on their Artisans and Master Artisans for their newsletter and press releases promoting their annual shows, I jumped at the opportunity. I have always had an interest in writing, history and art, so it seemed an obvious fit.

When I was again approached about a year ago to see if I might have interest in penning an entire book profiling each of the Roycroft Master Artisans, I was thrilled beyond belief, yet incredibly humbled. How could I possibly do justice to these amazing artists and their God-given talents?

And then the answer came to me. I truly believe that writing is an art, and every time I sit down to write I try to paint a mental picture for the reader. Using my "head, heart and hands," just as a Roycroft Artisan would — I construct a story with the hope that it touches the reader and leaves a lasting impression. I hope to connect with the reader's head and heart, and give them a treasure to hold in their hands.

Knowing their incredibly busy schedules — working, creating, traveling, mentoring — the toughest part in moving forward with this book was trying to figure out a way to make this an easy process for the artists while still keeping it interesting for the reader. With that in mind, I decided to write the profiles in a question-and-answer format. Each artist was given a list of twelve questions and were asked to answer the very first question — which was about their artistic specialty — and any other four questions from the list. The questions ranged from schooling and inspirations to artistic goals still to be fulfilled and notable career achievements. In doing so, I felt that most artists would likely select a different set of questions than those before or after them in the book, thereby making each profile unique and distinct.

Well, what I quickly discovered is that these artists really do like to think outside the box! While I am very pleased with the end result, you will see that some of our artists did not play by the rules. While the goal for each profile was somewhere between 1,000 and 1,200 words, you'll find that some are much shorter while others are much longer. You'll also notice that while some artists did indeed answer a total of five questions, others answered only a couple ... or chose to answer nearly every question.

I decided to just go with the flow and let them answer however they saw fit to answer. The result, I believe, are artist profiles that are as individual and unique as their works of art. I hope you enjoy reading them as much as I enjoyed crafting this unique piece to hold in your hands, feel with your heart and store in your head.

— *Joe Kirchmyer*

In 1976, a group of East Aurora residents with a common interest in the Roycroft Campus and the philosophy of Elbert Hubbard set in motion a plan to preserve those ideals which had made the campus a center of the Arts and Crafts Movement.

Some of the founding members of this core group were Nancy Hubbard, a granddaughter of Elbert Hubbard; Charles Hamilton, a historian and frequent author on Hubbard and the Roycroft; Kitty Turgeon, then innkeeper at the Roycroft; and Rixford Jennings, a local artist who grew up as a paperboy on Hubbard's campus. They, along with a meeting roomful of others, decided that this was something too important to let slip into the dust of an attic-bound history book.

After several meetings and energetic discussion, the Roycrofters-At-Large Association was formed. The bond they created was blessed by the spirit of Roycroft. Today the not-for-profit organization is still actively working to keep alive the history and philosophy of Roycroft through special events centered on and around the Roycroft Campus. Through the efforts of Kitty Turgeon and the organization, the campus became a National Historic Landmark. You are invited to come and visit East Aurora, New York, home of the Roycroft and the Roycrofters-At-Large Association ... and may the spirit of Roycroft be with you on your "little journey."

The Roycroft Mark — Old and New

The original Roycroft mark (the single "R") was trademarked by Elbert Hubbard in 1906. It is said to be older than recorded time — used by monks in the Middle Ages at the end of their hand-illuminated manuscripts signifying "The best I can do, dedicated to God."

Hubbard added the "R" symbolizing Royal Craft — Roycroft. In 1976, Rixford Jennings changed the design to incorporate two back-to-back Rs signifying the Roycroft Renaissance for the Roycrofters-At-Large Association.

The back-to-back "R" mark is Nationally Registered and may only be used by the organization's juried artisans.

How the Roycrofters-At-Large Association is Organized

The Roycrofters-At-Large Association is a 501(c)3 not-for-profit corporation administered by an elected board of directors. The board relies upon standing committees as defined by the bylaws. Members are also eligible to hold seats on the board and to participate in all committees.

For the past several years, membership in the organization has remained at about three hundred, with one-fourth (25 percent) of that number being juried Roycroft Renaissance Artisans, many who work out of their own studios. The non-artisans are people who wish to support and help promote the spirit and ideals of the original Roycrofters.

The Jury Process

To become a Roycroft Renaissance Artisan, a craftsman must be sponsored by a Master Artisan and submit pieces of his or her work to a jury comprised of Master Artisans.

Only artisans whose work exemplifies the following criteria will be awarded the use of the Roycroft Renaissance mark:

- High quality of hand craftsmanship
- Excellence in design
- Continuous artistic growth
- Originality of expression
- Professional recognition

There are two levels of juried craftsmen, the Artisan level and the Master Artisan level. All newly juried artisans will enter at the Artisan level and must re-jury annually. All Master Artisans must re-jury every five years. Artisans and Master Artisans will have equal use of the Roycroft Renaissance mark and are eligible to be offered the opportunity to make one of the patron membership premiums offered each year.

There is also an Artisan Emeritus designation which, upon approval of the Master Jury and the board of directors, is bestowed upon a current Artisan or Master Artisan who is no longer able to physically produce his or her craft yet still is considered by peers to be a Roycroft Artisan in word and spirit.

For more information, please visit www.ralaweb.com.

History courtesy of the Roycrofters-At-Large Association website.

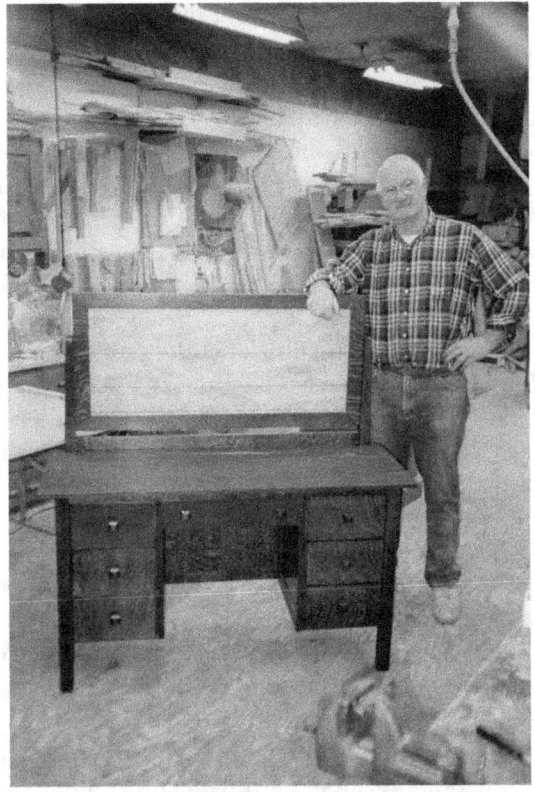

Describe your artistic specialty and what you typically like to create.

In August of 1994, I retired as principal of Clarence Center Elementary School. My wife was still teaching, so my days were spent cooking and cleaning which I tired of quickly. I called my friends Ben Little and Tom Harris, both Roycroft Master Artisans in wood, who owned a woodworking shop and asked them if they wanted a senior citizen volunteer. Their response was positive and that I should report to work right after Christmas.

Thus, in January 1995, my woodworking journey began. Initially I was asked to sweep floors, do some finish work, and assist with moving and delivering pieces that were under construction. I spent a lot of time watching and learning. It wasn't long before they asked me to make some of the small pieces that they sold in their Schoolhouse Gallery.

So under their careful watch and direction, the pieces were made (most of which came out fine). As I completed projects for them I began to think of pieces that I could make for myself. I now had a fair knowledge of the equipment and the different kinds of wood. My knowledge and progress was due totally to Tom and Ben's willingness to mentor me on the necessary woodworking skills and techniques.

In the fall of '95, one of my sons asked me to build him a glass-front bookcase and place it on a two-door chest. I wanted a project but not something that large; however, I decided to try it. With a lot of help from Tom and Ben, by the end of my first year as a woodworker the project was completed. The look of pleasure when my son saw the piece was all I needed. I was hooked and ready to start another.

It didn't take long for the other two sons to realize that Dad could help them furnish their homes. I now had a new vocation — building furniture for my children, grandchildren and interested buyers. In the next 20 years I would build well over 300 pieces using cherry, maple, quarter-sawn oak and in-barked hickory. These included at least 15 beds, several dressers, tables, bookcases and couches. I would also become a Roycrofters-At-Large Artisan and Master Artisan through the jury process.

As I reflect over my last 50 years, it becomes obvious that the first 30 were entirely different from the last 20. As a building principal, my success was dependent upon my ability to develop and maintain an environment in which teachers were able to do their best work. They were the key to the success of the students. Thus, I was successful only when students were good citizens and achieved their maximum level.

A woodworking artisan is totally dependent on his or her ability to come up with an idea, develop a design, make a scale drawing, select the wood, build the project and apply the finish. If the project does not come together because of poor planning or a building mistake, it is the artisan's fault. But it is only time and money. As a principal, poor planning or mistakes might affect the teachers' ability to do their job, which in turn affects the lives of the students.

There is also a difference in the rewards that one receives in the two professions. Regardless of how good your school is, there is not much positive feedback to the principal. As an artisan, if you build a beautiful piece, the receiving person lets you know immediately what their feelings are. The best reward comes when I build something for a grandchild and he or she says, "Thank you, Grandpa," and gives me a big hug. Personally, I also receive a great deal of satisfaction when I go into my children's homes and see the many pieces of furniture that are in daily use. Most of the pieces have the double R mark signifying they were made by a Roycroft artisan.

In summary, my woodworking projects have given me a great deal of satisfaction as I made use of my head, heart and hands.

Who/what are your inspirations, and why?

I will be forever grateful for the willingness of Tom Harris and Ben Little to spend hours teaching, coaching and helping me to become the artisan that I am. I will also be grateful to the other Roycroft Artisans whose media is wood. The outstanding workmanship of Thomas Pafk inspires me to always work toward perfection. Thomas Moser, president and founder of Thomas Moser Cabinet Makers Co., has been a great inspiration to me. He was trained at Geneseo College, became an educator at Bates College in Maine and started making furniture in his spare time. He ultimately became president of a worldwide furniture company. I spoke with Mr. Moser at a fine furniture show and two things he said caught my attention. They are, "Nothing goes out the door unless it's perfect," and "The back must look as good as the front."

I live in East Aurora in a Roycroft woodworker-built home. Their excellent craftsmanship and use of wood inspire me each day to follow in their footsteps.

What is your attraction to the Roycroft arts community and the Roycrofters-At-Large Association? How has it impacted you as an artist?

The Roycrofters-At-Large Association came to life in 1976. Prior to this, interest in the Roycroft was minimal. As a result of the organization's leadership efforts, a revival began to occur and interest in joining the group increased. A brand was developed (double R).

Artisans became a part of the group. The history of the Roycroft and Hubbard was given to the community. My first real knowledge of the association came about when I became a woodworker. Once that happened, I wanted to become part of the artisan group. However, their standards were such that I didn't think I could qualify. It wasn't until the year 2000 that I submitted my work for the masters to jury and was pleased when I received their approval. I was now a Roycroft Artisan and a proud member of an elite group who were the major force in keeping the spirit of the Roycroft alive. It is my firm belief that had it not been for the birth of the Roycrofters-At-Large Association, Roycroft would not be alive today.

Please share something else related to your craft which was not on this list of questions.

After I retired from Clarence Center School and became a woodworker, I built and donated two pieces of furniture that remain a part of the school library. One is a coffee table for kids to kneel at and read their books. On the top of the table I inscribed the words, "Knowledge is Power." The second piece is a display case which houses children's private collections, artwork or other projects. It was dedicated in memory of Peter Greatbatch who was the director of the East Hill Foundation. The foundation had donated funds to the Clarence Center Library which were used to automate the card catalog and supply several computers for the library. Each time I return to visit the school a feeling of pride and joy come over me as I observe the children around those two pieces. The children may not remember that I was a principal, but they will enjoy two things that I created for them.

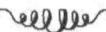
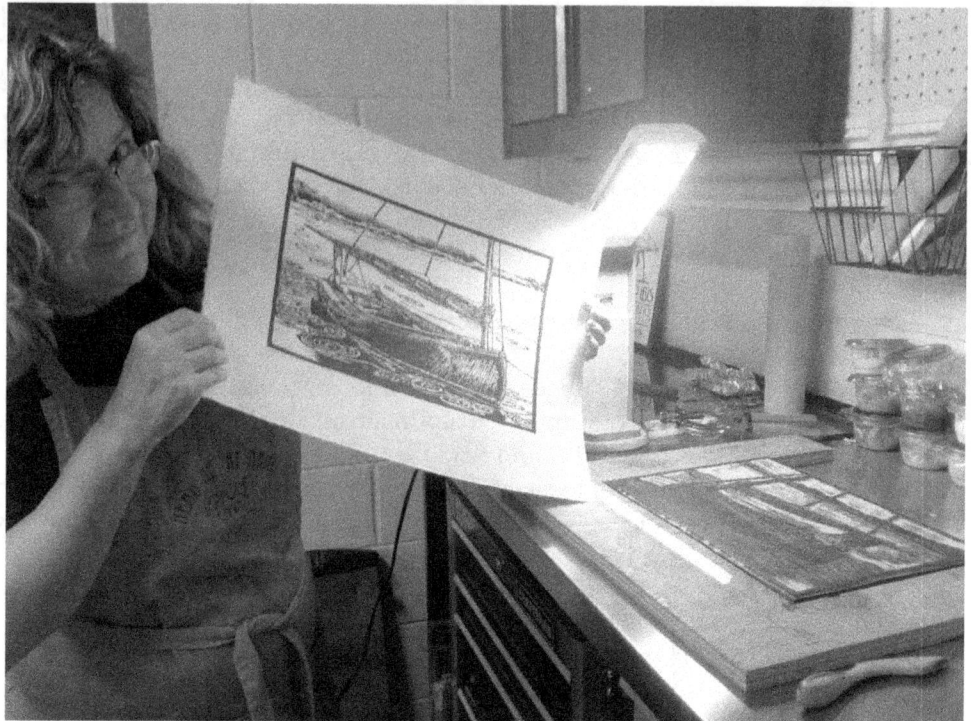

Describe your artistic specialty and what you typically like to create.

I'm a traditional printmaker working in carved linoleum blocks for relief printing and copper plate etching and mezzotints as well, all in oil-based inks. I've been a graphic designer and illustrator by trade for decades, and block prints are a natural fit for me as a designer while my etchings are the perfect outlet for my first love, pen-and-ink illustration.

Subject matter for my block prints is mostly maritime, which is a little unusual for printmakers working in the Arts and Crafts Movement arena, then and now. Traditional subject matter in the Arts and Crafts Movement covers a lot of ground but it's mostly landscape. There's comparatively very little in the way of boats. I'm a lifelong sailor and I love sailing traditional small craft. Some of my best customers are sailors and I strive for accuracy in the boats I portray, even in those simplified, carved linoleum lines.

I reserve my more personal work, however, for my etchings and mezzotints. For those I'm generally doing more mythic and natural world subject matter — fairytales, Greek and Celtic myths, and native Florida plants and animals for the most part. Intaglio etching, which I first learned as an elective in college, can give you such an elegant line. I love how forgiving copper is too. I never would have believed it until I tried it.

Who/what are your inspirations, and why?

I went to the Two Red Roses Foundation's 2008 woodblock exhibit at the nearby Leepa-Rattner Museum of Art in Tarpon Springs, Florida. In fact, I went back twice to see it. I was smitten by what I saw there. I had already started taking some relief printing classes at the Dunedin Fine Art Center as a break to get off of the computer. As I was already familiar with the history of the English and American Arts and Crafts Movement, I knew I wanted to catch this show but this was the first time I'd ever seen original block prints from the era. I loved everything about them — the contrast, the beautiful color palettes and graphic qualities, the Japanese influence and the overall emphasis on good design. I started trying to incorporate that look and feel in my work. In fact, it was two of my sailboat prints, "Melonseed Skiff" (2008) and "Catboat" (2009), which first really reflect the Arts and Crafts influence in my linoleum block printing.

I love the Pre-Raphaelites and late 19th and early 20th century illustration, particularly the work of Arthur Rackham, Elizabeth Shippen Green, Howard Pyle, Jessie Wilcox Smith, Franklin Booth and so on. I also really admire contemporary illustrators such as Charles Vess, Omar Rayyan and Rebecca Guay. My personal work reflects that love of earlier period illustration and also newer fantasy work.

Describe the space where you typically create, and what is so special about that place?

I'm really fortunate to have two studios. My main studio is where I work out of in the house. I still do freelance design so I have a full array of all of the computer equipment that goes with digital design and illustration today. But on the other side of the room is a large drafting table that I bought from my former TV station employer for pennies on the dollar before I left there in 1999. I do all of my preliminary block print and etching design work on that — all of the scribing and carving too — mainly while listening to audiobooks. It's a great place to work with large windows, a nice view of the yard and plenty of light.

I have a standing 22 x 35-inch Blick Master Etch Model II etching press that I bought from another local printmaker who was moving to New York City and didn't want to ship his press north. It's impossible to keep a press like that from rusting in garages down here in Florida, so in 2009 my husband and I built a combination studio and storage building in the back yard that also just happened to be the first privately owned, certified Category 5 hurricane shelter in the county. It's a no frills block and steel building but it's air conditioned and a comfortable, productive place to work with no distractions.

What is your attraction to the Roycroft arts community and the Roycrofters-At-Large Association? How has it impacted you as an artist?

Though I live in Palm Harbor, Florida, my husband was born and raised in Buffalo and Tonawanda, New York, and we've made frequent visits up there. I fell in love with the Roycroft Campus and East Aurora the first time I visited, or should I say the idea of it, as there wasn't much to see back in the early 1990s. But I did see the work of Roycroft Artisans in the Copper Shop gallery there. That led to finding information about how to become a Roycroft Artisan right about the time I started working on linoleum block prints in earnest in 2009. I applied to the Roycroft jury for the first time a year later.

Every artist these days needs a niche to stand out from the crowd and I started to make more sales after I picked up a more Arts and Crafts look to my work. At the same time, it's something I'm genuinely passionate about; the change in direction was not made simply for the sake of marketing. It was a very good path to take in my new career as an exhibiting artist.

The double "R" mark has been surprisingly recognizable down here in Florida and has been responsible for more great conversations in my booth and increased sales than I would have imagined. We have so many Western New York visitors during our primetime outdoor art show season down here in October through March. They know about Roycroft and they know what the mark signifies. Tampa Bay actually has quite a large inventory of Arts and Crafts bungalows and the Two Red Roses Foundation is currently building the fantastic new Museum of the American Arts And Crafts Movement (MAACM) an hour from my home down in St. Petersburg. It's a great time to be aligned with the Arts and Crafts revival down here and I'm honored to be known as a Roycroft Master Artisan in Tampa Bay.

Where can people see and/or purchase your art?

I'm delighted that the Copper Shop on the Roycroft Campus, where I saw Roycroft Artisan work for the first time and where I decided then and there to become one, is now offering my block prints and etchings. I'm also represented by Craftsman House Gallery in St. Petersburg, Florida, and the Clay and Paper Gallery in Dunedin, Florida. I'm in the process of setting up e-commerce online right now, but until that's ready my work can be seen at www.studioibis.com and I can be contacted from there.

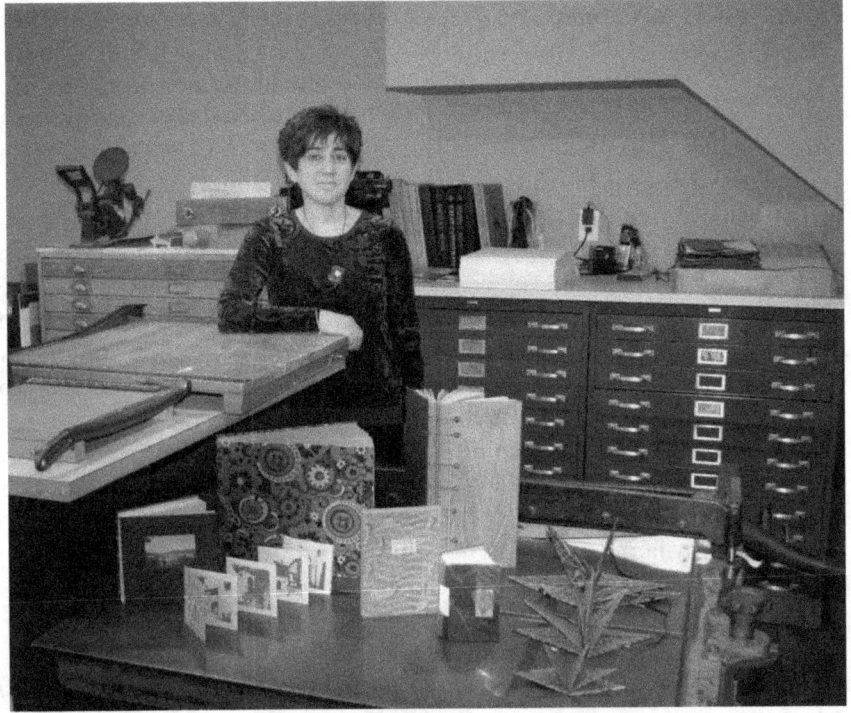

Describe your artistic specialty and what you typically like to create.

My mark is in book arts. I make functional books that serve a variety of purposes such as artists' sketchbooks, writing journals, special occasion books and one-of-a-kind presentation books. I also use the idea of the book as an art form. These artists' books include sculptural books, books that combine word and image, books without words and small edition printed books. Integrated in many of my books are the hand-painted paste papers and marbled papers that I love to make.

Who/what are your inspirations, and why?

In my first design class at Buffalo State College I was introduced to the book as an art form by my professor, Lynne McElhaney. I became intrigued by books and paper and have loved making them ever since. I was an apprentice bookbinder at the Soleil Bookbindery in Rochester, N.Y., where I was trained to make traditional books.

I was inspired to become a Roycrofter by Dorothy Marker, a Roycroft emeritus in printmaking. Dorothy was taking my bookmaking classes as I was taking her printmaking classes. She suggested that I think about becoming a Roycrofter. I knew that to be a Roycrofter, one had to be excellent at one's craft. When Dorothy suggested becoming a Roycrofter, I contacted the first person that I knew who could teach me more. Lynne had since retired as a professor but was willing to mentor me.

In more recent years, I have had the good fortune to study with Donald Dehoff, a local bookbinder who has taught me binding, foil stamping and book restoration. The idea of working towards becoming a Roycrofter was a great inspiration for broadening my knowledge, researching and exploring other aspects of book arts. I continue my study and take courses to further my study.

Describe the space where you typically create, and what is so special about that place?

My studio is in the basement of my home. I have always had a studio in the basement of wherever I have lived, including the house where I grew up. My current studio is a wonderful space that my husband has moved and redesigned a few times. Originally, the space was his wood shop. He traded sides of the basement with me so I could have better light with the large windows and more space.

I originally used my studio space to teach bookmaking classes at home, as well as a personal studio space. I now have a working fireplace and places for visitors to sit in front of the fire along with my bookbinding equipment and work tables. My studio houses bookbinding equipment, work tables, book presses, a sewing frame and flat files. A 100-year-old board shear, which is like "a paper cutter on steroids" used for cutting book board, and a job backer are the two fairly recent additions to my studio that have made my work so much more efficient.

On a sunny day there is so much natural light coming in from the large windows that I sometimes do not need to turn on the overhead lighting. It is a special place for me as it houses all the materials I have collected over time to create my work and it is a space that my family spends time with me as they create works of their own or things we work on together. My husband has worked very hard to design a great space for me to work.

Please share something else related to your craft which was not on this list of questions.

I consider myself a teaching artist. I am not an artist or craftsperson that travels to many shows. I mostly make one-of-a-kind artworks that have been commissioned or pieces generated from my own ideas. I find teaching other people the art of making books very fulfilling. No matter what age or level of teaching, I have always found a way to use books.

Throughout my career I have taught art in a variety of capacities. I have taught at the elementary, secondary and college levels, and I have taught numerous workshops across Western New York. Whether I am teaching a corporate workshop, a Girl Scout troop or a group of adults, making books offers endless possibilities for creating art. Books are familiar to all of us and making your own gives students a sense of accomplishment and an innovative way to learn information in various subject areas.

Teaching the art of books to others allows me to interact with people of all ages who are inspired by the book form. I enjoy demonstrating something most people have never made before, and seeing their reaction with the result is gratifying and inspiring!

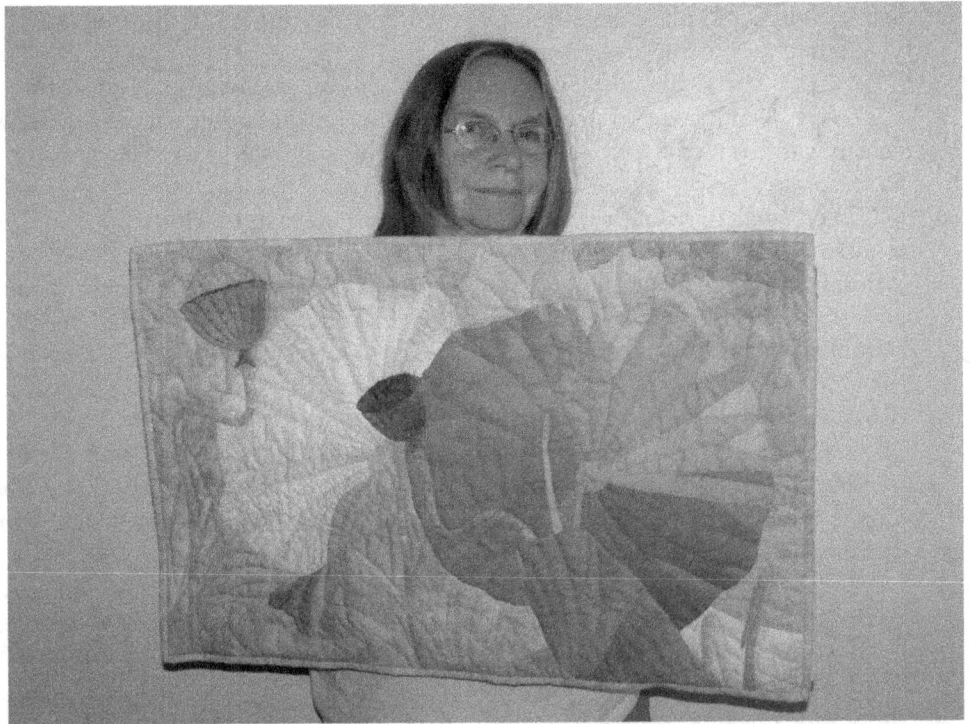

Describe your artistic specialty and what you typically like to create.

I work in textiles, and most of my pieces begin with closely woven plain white cotton fabric. I color pieces of the fabric with fabric paint and use this fabric with handprints and sun prints of leaves and other natural materials.

I print leaves with black fabric ink onto white cotton. This leaves an impression of veins — I do both sides of the leaf, which gives a right-hand and a left-hand image. As I slide a baren over the leaf, I can vary the pressure and direction of movement, emphasizing different parts and textures of the leaf. When cured and fixed, these images are colored with fabric paint and again heat fixed. I cut out the leaves, baste seam allowances and hand-applique to plain painted fabric to build up a surface.

For sun printing, I press flattened weeds or leaves onto a still-damp and stretched painted piece of cloth. This is exposed outdoors to sunlight. When dry, a negative image is revealed when the plant material is removed. This image can be somewhat controlled by varying moisture and exposure. This too must be heat fixed.

Larger wall pieces are inspired by photographs I've taken of natural sites. A photo is enlarged and then refined, and irrelevant details are removed. Other elements are added or moved, then I create a cartoon which I cut up to mark fabric, which must fit together correctly. I hand-piece and applique, and no adhesive is used.

For pillows and bags, smaller images are used. The finished object is built around the images, usually with hemp or linen fabric. I assemble bags and pillows with a sewing machine.

Who/what are your inspirations, and why?

My work is inspired by the growth and change of natural surroundings, including the "urban forest." For me, here in the seasonal Northeast, plants and leaves carry a sense of time and place, and their growth following simple rules produces a proliferation of forms and colors.

I visit many local natural places in every season, photographing sites and collecting, identifying and preserving leaves, flowers and other natural materials. This activity has revealed much information that is new to me, even having grown up in Erie County, New York.

Even small parts of the landscape expand when seen up close. Some of my wall pieces have shown small things magnified. A large view of crown vetch — clover-sized ground cover — brought to mind a passionflower. Horsetails, a primitive plant found at Sinking Pond locally, is a present-day relative of the tree-sized Calamites that dominated Paleozoic forests. The same rules of growth affect the small, even leaves of the ginkgo that graces the north side of the Roycroft Campus and the large, much-dissected leaves of a ginkgo two blocks from my home.

My plant heroes are Albrecht Dürer and his "Great Piece of Turf" and Peter Del Tredici of the Arnold Arboretum. Not only did he discover wild-growing ginkgo in China, but he granted a pardon to weeds in his book "Wild Urban Plants of the Northeast."

Describe the space where you typically create, and what is so special about that place?

I work everywhere, but as I depend on sunlight, summer is the best time to work. My studio is therefore movable. In the winter I work in the living room, where the sewing machine I use for finishing small pieces sits in view of the TV.

Between equinoxes I work outdoors when possible. In early spring I collect young herbaceous shoots and leaves decayed into skeletons over the winter, and in late fall newly fallen leaves can be found not only in woods but in Delaware Park's arboretum.

Summer sunlight is perfect for printing these leaves and shoots. I can pin painted fabric on foam board palettes, roll leaves onto them and spread any number of them to dry in the sun. The decayed leaves reveal not only veins and holes, but some show their internal layers.

The flow of paint as it is drying also produces unforeseeable patterns as it is folded, salted and tilted. In the morning I can mix colors in the shade of the shed and arrange materials on the board without the paint beginning to set. The development of an image depends both on heat and light. As the day goes on and sun falls on the front of the house, boards can be placed on the front steps as I complete cleanup by hosing off my work table and myself.

Working outdoors has its own surprises, of which one of the best was a set of wasp footprints across a drying leaf print. Pragmatically, It drastically increases the quantity, speed and size of my output.

What is your attraction to the Roycroft arts community and the Roycrofters-At-Large Association? How has it impacted you as an artist?

I always admired the Roycroft community for its commitment to crafts of the highest quality, solid workmanship and well-conceived design. They showed work that was both useful and beautiful. The historic campus, with its ties to Western New York, my home, also attracted me.

When I was not affiliated with the association I had the opportunity to exhibit many times in the summer show. This was a great chance to see what Roycroft Artisans were creating. I always hoped for good weather so the woodworking and furniture could be displayed outside. When looking at the products of Roycroft Artisans I always thought, "I wish I had made that."

Since I have been a Roycroft Artisan, I have tried to make every year a step up in craftsmanship and creativity while also being more critical of my own work. It's become less dismaying to redo or reimagine a piece if the outcome will be better. Finally, I can relax when displaying my work to others knowing I've put everything into it and that it has integrity.

When someone looks at something you have created, what type of reaction or emotion do you hope to see, and why?

Aside from the instant validation of a person wanting to take home an item I've produced, I think I'd like them to slow down and look for a while with real interest. If there are questions to be answered, even better. I would like to see some recognition of an image, a place, a technique.

If it seems the person has been mentally following the steps I took in creating the piece, I am also happy. I am happy when a person who asks to touch a piece realizes that the surface has been layered and constructed, and that it is "real."

However, for me the best thing is to be asked if I could teach the viewer some of the same techniques. I love to see the look on the face of someone who's picking a leaf that they have pressed into the wet paint, exposed to sun and dried. Discovering the image produced is exciting and addictive.

I've been teaching traditional quilting at the Amherst Center for Senior Services for over 20 years, which is longer than I thought I would, and it's still rewarding to see each student pursue and finish a project in her own unique way.

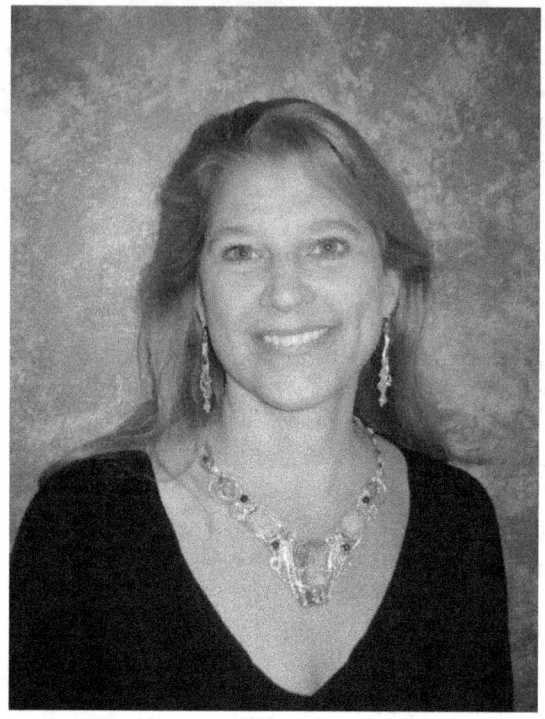

Describe your artistic specialty and what you typically like to create.
I am a Roycroft Renaissance Master Artisan in jewelry.

Describe when you first truly realized that you had artistic skills, and how you worked to develop those skills.

My background in arts and crafts began as a child and was nurtured when I was very young. As my parents recognized that I had artistic talent, they began sending me for private art lessons. When I was young my passion was for watercolor painting, but I was blessed to be nurtured in different types of arts in high school and college. While attaining a business and marketing college degree I worked in my family's construction company and drew blueprints and designed kitchen interiors. My hobbies included porcelain painting and glass fusing in a kiln for making jewelry. Later I learned copper foil stained glass techniques.

While my children were young I began to sell my items at the local craft shows so that I could stay home and raise my children. I turned my miniature paintings into jewelry and these items were well received by the public, thus starting my current business as a jeweler in 1995. I experimented with different techniques and taught myself the technique of wire wrap setting in jewelry.

I really enjoy working in this type of jewelry setting. The challenge of this wire wrap technique of setting is in working with thin pieces of square sterling silver and gold-filled wire of various gauges. Each wire is banked, twisted, bent and crimped with various shaped pliers. However, my favorite tool for maneuvering the metal is my right thumbnail, and most work is simply done by maneuvering the metal with my fingers. I consider this technique almost like weaving with the thin pieces of metal.

Typically, I design as I go, bending and banking the metal and incorporating beads and pearls into the design. I work with many stones right in front of me, and on the most challenging multi-stone pieces, I draw the layout and placement of stones.

I love working on non-symmetrical and unusually cut stones that are not round or oval in shape. I also continue to make some of the stones myself in a four-firing kiln process using glass, porcelain and gold leaf. In addition, I hand-paint floral designs with overglaze on small porcelain stones, kiln fire them multiple times, and then hand set them. I know a piece is complete when I look at it in a mirror to see if it is balanced both in viewing it straight on and in reverse.

Another challenge of a wire-wrapped setting for jewelry is blending both stability and wearability of the piece especially when it has multiple stones. In addition, my goal is to create a piece of jewelry that is truly unique. I achieve this in shopping for the unusual stones and gemstones and then setting each piece individually, working directly on the stone. No mold is made; there is only one.

I hand-pick affordable stones to give my clients not just a piece of wearable artwork, but a reasonably priced one as well. Also, I listen to my customers' requests for color and stones and continually add to my line. When a customer asks me what I have that is new, I can then show him or her many items.

Custom orders are gladly done, from weddings to setting the collected treasures of my customers. As I create a setting, I work towards their desires in shape so as to create a memory for them. This technique of setting can incorporate fragile items such as shells or glass because there is no heat used in the process.

Some of the most interesting items that people bring me are things such as their grandmother's chipped tea cups which I cut, grind and set so they can wear a little part of it as an heirloom. The most unusual items that I have set include Indian arrowheads, coal and fish bones. All have sentimental value, especially to the one wearing them.

Do you travel from show to show? What are the best and worst aspects of life on the road? Feel free to share your most memorable story.

Even though the system of putting up and taking down my booth is relatively efficient, the show vendor life has its challenges. One on the most memorable shows was when a waterspout touched down near the booths at a Finger Lakes show. I was so happy to have my husband with me. He held down the tent as the wind blew many booths away. I have also had my tent roof collapse down on me in a rainstorm. At another show I opened it in the morning to discover that people had slept in my booth at night for shelter. So, each show has its memories, but most of all, I love talking with people. In the course of this type of business, you make a lot of nice friends.

What is your attraction to the Roycroft arts community and the Roycrofters-At-Large Association? How has it impacted you as an artist?

As I continue producing jewelry as an artist, there have been influencing people and organizations that have impacted how I do my craft. I have been mentored as an artist within the Roycroft community. The helpful exchange of advice and constructive critique of my work over the years from other Roycroft Master Artisans has driven me to create new designs.

In addition, over the years I have learned that each piece is to be viewed as a piece of artwork and not just a piece of jewelry to sell. I believe that being subject to the jury process as an artist keeps the body of artists continually striving for a higher level of achievement not only in the craft, but in the way we represent the craft. Within the group of Roycroft Artisans, especially among the jewelers, there is a sense of camaraderie. I find that even though some of these artisans are my competition, they are my support group as well, and we treat each other with respect for each other's talent.

As an artist, some of the most significant achievements have been receiving the Roycroft Renaissance Master Artisan title and winning the Allentown Purchase Award. It has been very nice to win awards in various shows over the years, and it confirms that the effort in making my jewelry is recognized. Having the Roycroft Renaissance Master Artisan designation is one that I have worked toward for a number of years. The strict jury process, again, drives me as an artist to be meticulous and precise. And, when a particular piece wins an award, it's exciting and fun to be competitive in that sense as well.

Where can people see and/or purchase your art?

Some of my jewelry is listed on my website, as well as my show schedule, at www.pattycancillaart.com. But, I have found that people like to touch the pieces and try them on, so most of my jewelry is sold in the Western New York and Pennsylvania art shows.

When someone looks at something you have created, what type of reaction or emotion do you hope to see, and why?

I want my customers to be noticed and complimented when they wear my jewelry so that they really feel good about themselves. And, I want them to know that the piece is truly unique. I love when people tell me they came to a show just to see me. When people see my work, I would like them to say, "Wow! I have never seen anything like this," and then be able to afford it.

Please share something else related to your craft which was not on this list of questions.

I believe that my business is more than just making and selling jewelry, it's about building relationships. When my work and sales are going well, I am filled with a sense of being blessed by God and humbled that people would buy the work of my hands. I want to give credit to God for any talent that I have, for the income from my business and the achievement along the way.

In looking toward the future, my plans are to continue to develop beautiful new jewelry designs, perfect the craft as best I can and build new friendships along the way.

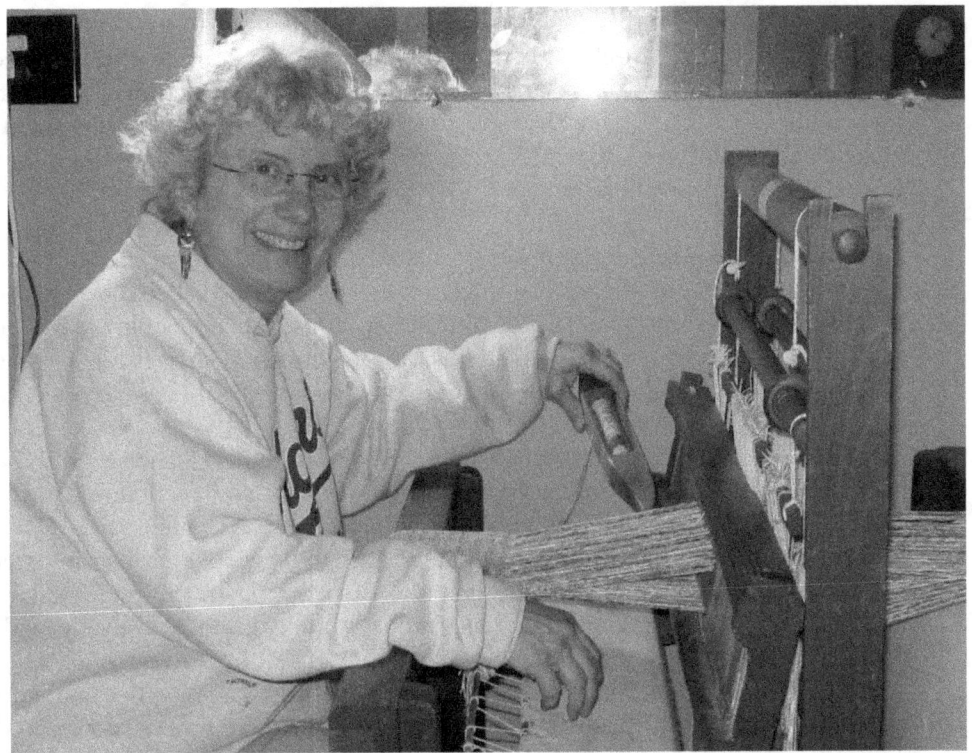

Describe your artistic specialty and what you typically like to create.

I am a handweaver and I create functional items, mostly scarves, shawls and other wearables. I really love using silks and rayons for their wonderful hand (drape) and sheen, and I sometimes use cotton, bamboo, alpaca and other wools, and occasionally other yarns.

As time passes I find myself using finer yarns than I ever thought I would. Although doing so involves much more time to create each piece, it also allows me to weave a cloth that is both lighter weight and has more design elements. I also love weaving lace and making fabric that has planned "holes" or areas where threads move aside to create textures and patterns.

The name of my business is Second Wind Weaving. This name reflects the fact that I came to this particular endeavor later in my life and gives some insight into other aspects of my weaving as well. I own two vintage floor looms that I use for almost all my weaving.

My first loom, a four-harness counterbalance loom, was handmade, likely in the 1930s or '40s. When I bought it, the loom had not been used in decades and required lots of time, TLC, and the replacement of all cords and string heddles. But this loom was clearly well-loved by its prior owner, who taped a little poem to the top roller bar. I've left it there as it is as true for me as it was for her:

My simple pleasures,
my gentle joys
weave a lovely pattern

of contentment in my life.

I purchased my second loom, an eight-harness Macomber loom, some years later. This loom was literally in pieces in a woman's (fortunately very dry) barn. Again, lots of hours of care and attention were needed to bring it back to functioning. Armed with the loom's serial number I contacted the Macomber company and learned that my loom left the factory on Veteran's Day, 1956. That bit of knowledge gave me goosebumps, because I knew that before it got to the barn this loom had spent much of its life at the Buffalo VA, teaching veterans how to weave as part of their therapy. A great connection if you ask me.

Describe the space where you typically create, and what is so special about that place?

I work at home in a space that might euphemistically be called a weaving studio. It's a room that's about 13 x 15 feet and used to house a piano, a big old desktop computer and lots of vinyl record albums. It has a bunch of shelves for my many bins of yarn, but not enough. I have bins stored in two other rooms as well. A weaver must have a big stash, you know. LOL.

As floor looms go, both of mine are small — the counterbalance is only about 30 inches wide, and the Macomber about 40 inches wide — so they fit into that space without a problem. The biggest drawback is that there's very little natural light so I have to rely on floor lamps that I move from here to there and back again to try and give me good light on the loom and the piece I'm working on at the moment.

I have a really nice porch right outside the "studio," but unfortunately neither of my looms moves much, especially the Macomber — it doesn't move at all. I have actually moved my little handmade loom out to the porch a few times but ended up with other problems I hadn't anticipated issues like glare and wind, so I won't do that again.

My house is on the market, and when it sells one of the "must haves" for my next home is space for a good weaving studio with great natural light.

Where can people see and/or purchase your art?

I've been doing a lot of custom weaving for the past few years, so I haven't been able to build up enough stock to have my work in stores or The Copper Shop on the Roycroft Campus. I do a small number of shows each year: the two RALA shows, a show or two at the Chautauqua Institution, and usually one or two more. Weaving is a slow process and I can't produce enough to do any more shows than that.

I do have a website I sell from — www.handwovenscarves.com — although it is in desperate need of updating. I have to decide between weaving and updating my website, and weaving wins 99 percent of the time. When my house sells I think that there will be a period of time when I'll be between places and won't have access to my looms; that's when I'll spend time updating my website.

My custom work for the past few years has been mostly handwoven baby wraps. So far I've shipped my baby wraps to nine states, three Canadian provinces and seven other foreign countries including Malaysia, Australia and New Zealand. Most of my baby wrap customers find me through either word of mouth or from my blog: www.secondwindjewelry.com/jewelry-weaving-blog.

When someone looks at something you have created, what type of reaction or emotion do you hope to see, and why?

I want people to be compelled to touch my weaving, to rub it between their fingers or against their cheeks, and to be thrilled with its softness and drape. I want them to wrap it around their necks and love the way it looks and feels. I want them to be able to envision it with their little black dress, or their winter coat, or their boyfriend's jacket, or over mom's shoulders or wrapped around their baby.

I want people who come into my booth to ask questions about fiber, thread count and the weaving process. I want them to recount their experiences weaving in grade school, high school or college. There are lots of people in this region who took weaving classes years ago at Buffalo State College.

I want them to tell me about their great-grandmother who wove everything from curtains to rag rugs for her house, or their neighbor who raises sheep and then spins and weaves or knits with their wool.

I want them to ask me where they can take weaving classes or what kind of loom they should buy. I want them to tell me about the loom they used to own but sold, or how they hope to get back to weaving when they retire.

While I do want to sell my work, far more than that I want communication. I want to inspire memories or spur creative juices.

Please share something else related to your craft which was not on this list of questions.

I really like bringing my art — weaving — to the public and encouraging community participation. In the summer of 2013 I worked with a local farmers' market. I built a simple 4- x 4-foot loom on site and got people who came to buy healthy fruits and veggies to weave. Little kids, teenagers, moms, dads and grandparents all tried their hand, creating a somewhat ethereal piece. When it was done the weaving hung in front of a store in town for a season. It was great!

In 2014 I was awarded an Artist in the Community grant through the Cattaraugus County Arts Council, funded in part by the New York State Arts Council. I had a great time with this, bringing weaving to the public in ways they wouldn't have considered.

First, I worked with the elementary art teacher. Every child in grades three through five worked on a small loom made from stiff cardboard and Styrofoam. The children chose colors of yarn and created small woven pieces, about two inches square. In the end there were more than 300 little squares!

Then I partnered with the local library to use their outdoor space. I arranged for three outdoor concerts: classical, rock 'n' roll, and African drums. At each concert I set up my little rigid heddle loom and encouraged everyone, from 5 year olds to great-grandparents, to take a turn weaving. I had about three dozen yarns of various colors and textures to choose from.

One of the project goals was to see if the musical genre had any impact on the colors or textures people chose. I don't think it did, but we created a woven banner at each concert anyway.

At the end of the summer I hung all three banners and all 300-plus student-woven pieces out in front of the library for all to enjoy. They stayed in place through the winter, and by spring some of the yarn had degraded enough that I had to take everything down.

This summer I'll be demonstrating and encouraging hands-on participation at the Roycrofters-At-Large summer show.

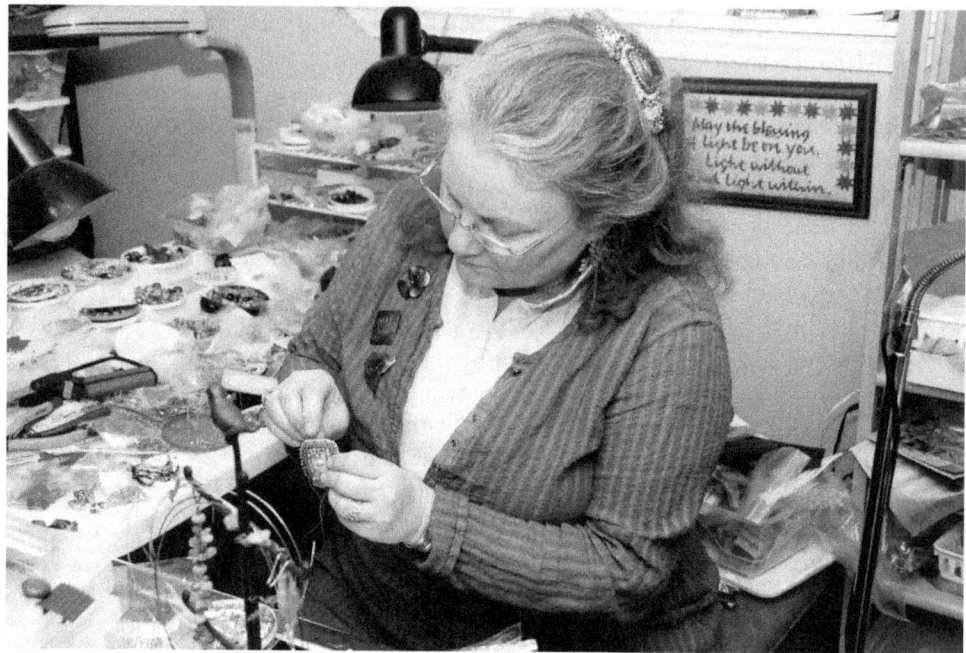

Describe your artistic specialty and what you typically like to create.

I was the first mark awarded for beadwork. I brought my love of beadwork and craftsmanship, with examples of sculpture, wall art and wearables (jewelry). With my master jury, I gave them wall art, wearables and sculpture.

Creating is a "drive." I need to create vessels, wall art, miniatures and wearable art, all my own designs. I love the needle and love the putting together of shapes and colors of beads. I use a mixed media to do beads; in the beginning mostly glass beads, and now I Incorporate many types of beads in many materials.

Describe the space where you typically create, and what is so special about that place?

I have a delightfully overcrowded and very busy studio in our home, yet the creating begins upon awakening. I am very grateful that God loves, loves, loves the creative process!

I have dressmakers' mannequins, I dress dolls (still) and I costume for theater (myself and my spouse).

Additionally, I collect different fibers, fabrics, textures, bird nests, dried branches from tomato vines, rocks, insect carcasses ... you see, almost everything has beauty and helps my creative process. I sketch, draw and watercolor my ideas. I also make patterns for my wearables and I will not make one piece that I wouldn't wear myself! Ah, ADD at its finest!

What is your attraction to the Roycroft arts community and the Roycrofters-At-Large Association? How has it impacted you as an artist?

To be associated with the Roycroft craftsmen and all their creativity is so energizing for me. I am very proud to be a Roycroft Master craftsman, to be an encouragement to other Roycroft craftsmen, to be encouraged, and to encourage future craftsmen. That is important to me, as is the association.

Everybody, and I do mean everybody, is good at something. God loves the creative process and everyone has something they are good at whether it's a craft, keeping a friend or doing a job. Everyone has a gift.

Being located in the Finger Lakes region I am unable to help the Roycrofters-At-Large Association as much as I would if I were closer. That is unfortunate for me.

As an artist, what is the best piece of advice that you were ever given? What words of inspiration or advice would you offer those who might aspire to follow in your artistic footsteps?

My mother and father encouraged me growing up — they were both creative — but the best encouragement or advice was from Dr. Daniel Goldsmith, one of my favorite professors at Hillsdale College in Hillsdale, Michigan. "Big Daddy" Goldsmith told me I was an artist who used fabrics (and beads) as one of my mediums and not to compare myself, my self worth and my creativeness with the 2-D art students. He told me, "Just as a woodworker uses a fine veneer, you use fabrics to create." In my heart I knew I was an artist but when I was that young I needed the encouragement!

As I stated above, everybody is good at something. I try to encourage all aspiring craftsmen, but art is work and to love it is not enough. One must constantly push themselves forward each day.

When someone looks at something you have created, what type of reaction or emotion do you hope to see, and why?

When you are creating, the joy is in the "doing." While a lot of people admire and may comment, it is the responsibility of the craftsman to educate the public, collector and buyer.

My head starts the creative process and my hands are still able to do the work. Yes, art is work, but my heart is in all I do and I do love my work!

My craft is ever evolving as I keep living and exploring the world around me. I never tire of seeing a beautiful dawn or a clever cat or my darling husband's smile. Then I pick up my sketchbook, head for my studio and begin the day again.

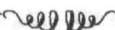

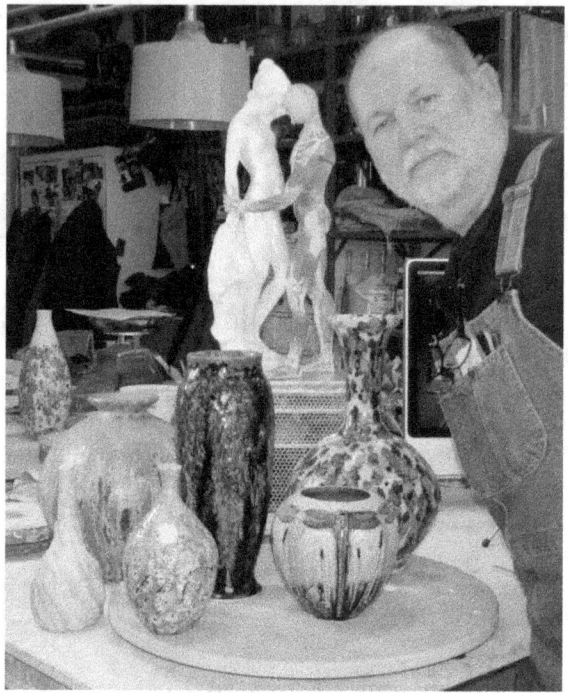

Describe your artistic specialty and what you typically like to create.

As a potter, my primary focus was always on beauty. A worthy endeavor surely. My pots are nature inspired, high-fired porcelain and depict nature that I see around me. I love to depict the weather, the season and time of day. I have made numerous rain pots, snow pots, wind pots, night pots and day pots. I love big full moons and bright suns often with each on opposite sides of the same pot.

Many pots will tell a story of sorts. One design might illustrate the "circle of life" around a given pot where a flower sprouts, grows, blooms, drops seeds and the seeds again sprout. Another pot might hint at the dilemma found in the Garden of Eden. At the same time, many pots are just about glaze, shape and color.

I have an Eastern aesthetic and love classic Asian shapes and images. I have seriously collected Japanese woodblock prints and frequently steal designs and images directly from them. That way, I can rationalize buying more of them. I think to myself, "Oh, I can use that image."

Another part of the attraction to Japanese prints is that my process of decorating a pot is in many ways very similar to the woodblock process. While the pursuit and production of "beauty" is an endless and worthy endeavor, lately I have been drawn to the human figure. Beauty is wonderful, but the depicted body and its implied consciousness means much more to me and I suspect, to all viewers.

Describe when you first truly realized that you had artistic skills, and how you worked to develop those skills.

In retrospect and in the recollections of people that grew up with me, I know I was always "artsy." I graduated from St. Louis University in 1970 in history and political science. However, it was not until 1973 that life took a sharp turn towards the arts. In the summer of '72, my future wife Kathy and I took a month long trip to the British Isles where we bummed around doing hostels and hitchhiking. To make a long story short, we crossed over to Amsterdam, bought an empty green 1966 VW Kleinbus, went to the flea market, outfitted it and drove to India and back spending 363 days on the road. That van is where we first started living together.

When that adventure ended — and what an adventure it was — suddenly the world looked different and my serious art adventure began. I had a painter take me under his wing and when I started hanging out with artists, I decided those were the kind of people I wanted to be around. After four years at a community college, I then moved to San Francisco and later graduated from the San Francisco Art Institute with a focus on sculpture.

I have always found working in three dimensions was easy for me, where working in 2D — painting, printing and the like — was difficult. For 10 years after SFAI, I painted realist paintings, made elaborate and expensive lamps depicting the history of various civilizations, and started buying buildings and fixing them up. Finally I had a cash flow that really freed me up.

I took a pottery class on a whim in 1993 and started making art pottery simply because I collected art pottery for years and that was what I was most familiar with. Keep in mind I was 44 years old and was artily developed. The first time I showed my pots, they were not priced. However, people insisted that I price them. I did, and they sold.

You know how it is when you get a cash flow because of something you like to do? I started making more elaborate and expensive pots. Fortunately, the web appeared just in time. I set up a website and things took off. I only physically showed and sold my pots for 10 years at one Ohio show called "Pottery Lovers." Otherwise, I was strictly web-based. When I noticed that dealers were my primary buyers, I quickly pushed prices to the retail limit. I am proud to say — in the finest Roycroft tradition — that I am a one-man shop and every pot I have made left my hands directly to the buyer. Never a gallery, never a middleman, though some dealers still bought retail and made money reselling!

Describe the space where you typically create, and what is so special about that place?

I was born and raised in St. Louis and when my future wife Kathy and I pulled back from California, we bought a large and beautiful commercial building in South St. Louis City. What used to be a grocery store became my studio and what used to be a barbershop became my office — one clean and one dirty room. The building we bought is big and we did not have much.

Because I was self-employed and set my own schedule, I became a compulsive collector and now have collections too numerous to mention. For many years I bought nearly anything made in the name of "art." After I had once again attended St. Louis Community College for five years — 1993 to 1998 — I decided to bite the bullet and spend $20,000 setting up a complete studio with two big stainless sinks, two wheels, three kilns, an expansive glaze kitchen, spray booth, etc. That was and still is my primary studio. I have since set up another studio in two more storefronts. However, my focus has changed from pure ceramics to more figurative sculpture — some still ceramic — but now the materials are whatever is necessary to make the point.

At this point I am engaged in producing a traveling show for a museum and it is a seven-year project. This project is strictly figurative, realist, obvious sculpture. Interestingly, I am forming a guild of mostly young, talented relatives that are working with me on this huge project. All my time and resources are directed to that end.

What is your attraction to the Roycroft arts community and the Roycrofters-At-Large Association? How has it impacted you as an artist?

I forget when I requested membership in the Roycrofters-At-Large Association. It has been a long time. What attracted me was the typical Roycroft ideal: Make honest, beautiful things yourself, and put those resulting objects in the hands of someone who loves them.

To date I have made approximately 1,500 pots. Virtually all my pots and sculptures are very clearly marked with "Tim Eberhardt, St. Louis, the date and the double RR logo" on the bottom. I add any info I please to the bottom of the pot so many pots have an extensive exhibition history, a personal comment or a greeting to a friend on the pot's bottom or inside. I am compulsive about providing accurate provenance for every piece. Collectors and historians love information.

As an artist, what has been your most significant achievement, or proudest moment, to date?

A couple unusual things I am proud of: I have never had a W-2, I have always been self-employed and I have always kept the best of my work. I have the best 250 pieces I have made. Of course I sold many, many pots I wish I had not, but you have to sell to get the image out. The beauty of being able to keep your best is when you are asked to show work, you have the best to show.

I no longer sell pots. I still make pots, just not as many, but don't sell. And in that guild mentality, I have talented throwers throw the pots now and I just decorate. My focus for the pots has changed from the more traditional art pottery where I impose my vision of nature on the pots to now, where I consider only the nature of the clay and the glaze and let them stand out on their own, rather than using the clay and glaze to illustrate nature.

There is still and always will be great joy in opening the kiln. It is perhaps a function of age and cash flow — I am 67 and comfortable — that I consider myself completely free to pursue any artistic desires. Lately, I have jokingly but seriously announced that, "I have left the church." The usual response to that statement is, "Which church?" To which I say, "All of them."

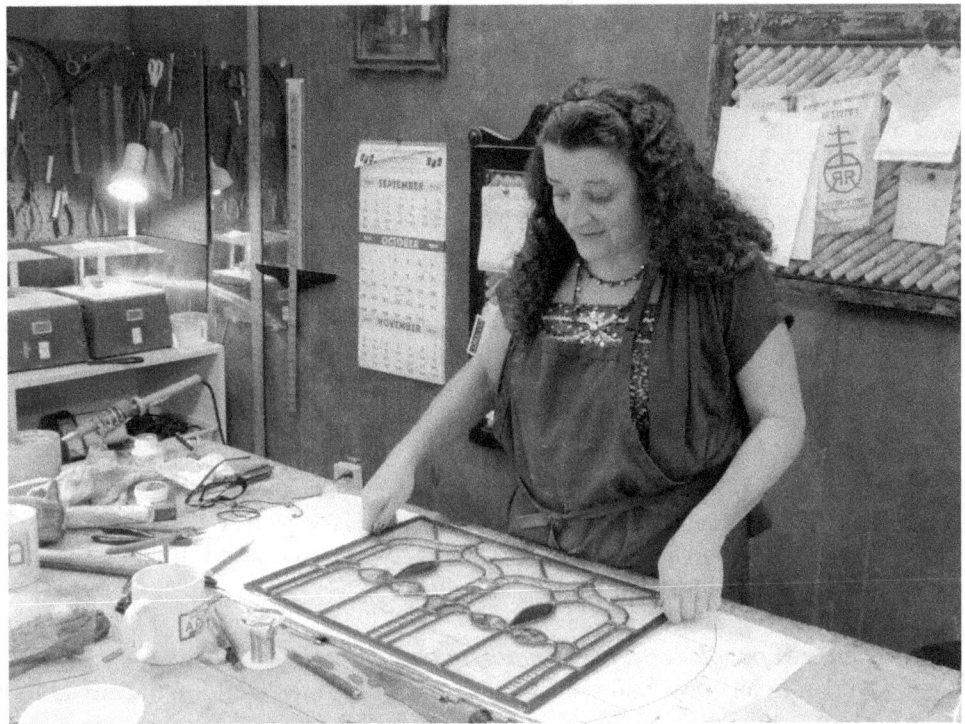

Describe your artistic specialty and what you typically like to create.

My speciality is stained glass, namely new creations for commissioned pieces. I work mainly with lead channels (the Old World method) and I am also well versed in the copper foil technique. I also specialize in the restoration of older leaded glass panels and have completed numerous projects in the area, for churches as well as private residences.

Describe when you first truly realized that you had artistic skills, and how you worked to develop those skills.

I have owned and operated a stained glass studio in the Village of East Aurora, New York, for over 30 years. I started experimenting with glass on my own, as my husband opened the "flat glass/auto glass" portion of the business. Being naturally curious and a bit artistic, I taught myself the basics of stained glass through trial and error, along with tons of books and old-time VHS tapes!

In the early 1980s I started teaching basic and advanced glass classes and was still learning right along with my students. I taught for about 15 years in "the shop," along with keeping up with custom orders. By the late 1990s I decided to give up teaching and focused more on custom commissioned pieces. Also during that time I offered my customers sandblasted designs on glassware and mirrors for commercial and private use.

What is your attraction to the Roycroft arts community and the Roycrofters-At-Large Association? How has it impacted you as an artist?

My attraction to the Roycroft arts community and the organization came about pretty naturally, as I was an established stained glass artist in East Aurora, had worked with numerous clients through the years, and had also collaborated with a few other Roycroft Artisans on various projects. The natural progression for me was to join a group of like-minded artisans who strive for excellence in their craft and are recognized by the community for their efforts.

As an artist, what is the best piece of advice that you were ever given? What words of inspiration or advice would you offer those who might aspire to follow in your artistic footsteps?

I was never really given any specific piece of advice about my art, although I was encouraged by teachers, family and friends to pursue my interest in stained glass. I had a major in art in high school and attended a BOCES program for commercial art during my last two years. I was accepted to Pittsburgh Art Institute in 1978, but never attended. I was dating my husband Arnie at the time, and the opportunity to open a glass shop in 1979 got the ball rolling with me creating in glass. After a few years I opened up the stained glass portion of Aurora Glass, and Aurora Art Glass was born.

My piece of advice is to concentrate on what you do best. If you love what you do and do it well, the rest will come naturally!

Where can people see and/or purchase your art?

People can come and visit at my studio which is located (on the circle) in East Aurora. I have part-time hours at the shop, and during those times I am always there. I don't sell items anywhere else but the shop, and even there I don't have a lot of items for sale as most everything that hits my work table is a custom design for a commissioned piece. I always encourage my customers to visit the shop as I do have items on display to help them visualize a finished piece. I also have design books and a large selection of glass for them to choose from.

I call what I do a "process" and tell my customers that they will meet with me at least one more time before we begin the project. They give me an idea and measurements, and I draw a design. They then come back to approve and/or make changes and pick out their glass choices and construction techniques and finishes. I also offer professional installation of finished pieces by my husband Arnie, who has been in the glass business for over 40 years. We truly are a one-stop glass shop.

As an artist, what has been your most significant achievement, or proudest moment, to date?

My most significant achievement has been the restoration of an entire church full of stained glass windows. The project, which spanned the course of two years, was completed in 2014. The original church located in West Seneca, New York, was crumbling down and needed to be totally rebuilt. The windows were harvested and stored on site until the construction of the new building would take place.

The new design of the church was implemented by the architect with a general knowledge of measurements of the available old windows. I was commissioned to resize, re-lead, re-cement and replace pieces of glass in 35 windows dating back to the original church, which was built in 1912.

The panels of Jesus and the angel, which adorn the front of the church on either side of the altar, were total "re-dos." The background glass surrounding the angel was totally replaced because the original glass did not match the rest of the background glass in the surrounding windows. The bell tower window which sits high above the altar and in the middle of the Jesus and angel windows was originally three separate panels. I reassembled the existing pieces and added new glass to make one large 57-inch diameter panel. It was quite the job to get it up and installed in one piece, but my husband Arnie promised it would go in without a hitch, and it did!

I was given artistic license during the whole project which was a blessing and made the whole experience very rewarding.

I should also mention my most heartfelt piece that I created during the time that my son was deployed to Afghanistan. Being a military mother in 2008 was a very difficult time in our lives for me and my husband, and we spent many a day worrying about the safety of our son during his deployment.

One day while reading The Buffalo News I spotted a picture of three soldiers who were looking for a lost comrade in Iraq. The emotion of the photograph prompted me to create the mosaic depiction of the peace I titled "The Weary Soldier." This piece depicts a soldier with his head resting in his hands upset with the fact that his battle buddy was still missing. Sandblasted details adorn the sleeves and wrist of the soldier and the unit patch was changed to reflect the New York National Guard symbol, which at the time my son was deployed with to Afghanistan.

This piece symbolizes every soldier that has been in combat, has been displayed in public many a time and his gotten recognition in the community. I eventually hope to create more moving pieces to reflect the emotion that many military families share. If I can connect with another mom, my effort will be all worth it. So I guess if I had a bucket list of projects to create before I can no longer do so, it would be a series of mosaics depicting the emotional interaction of soldiers and their families.

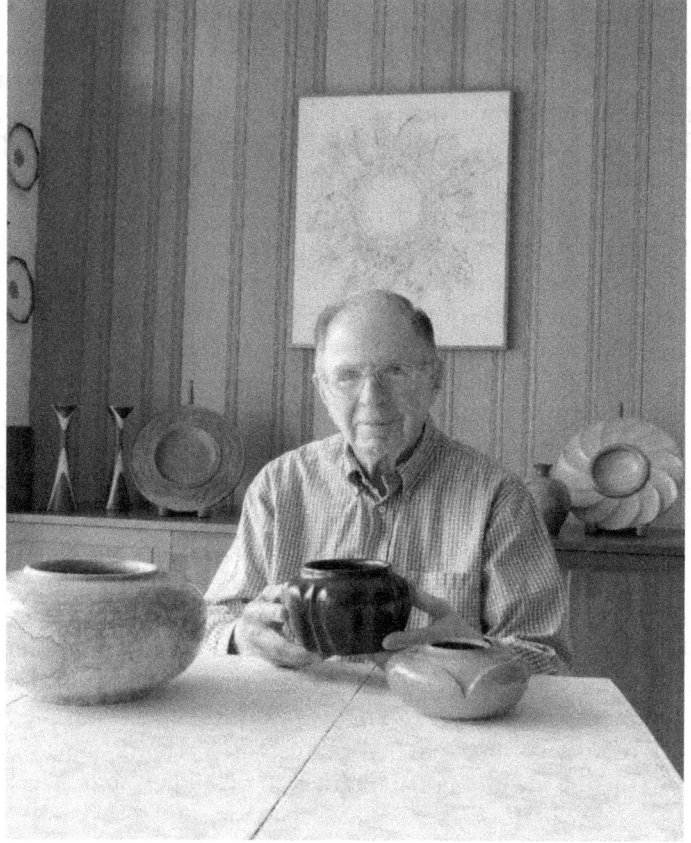

Describe your artistic specialty and what you typically like to create.

Woodworking has been a hobby of mine for many years. Over the years I have made a major effort to develop my skills with a particular focus on the creative aspects of woodturning. My pieces are characterized by clean designs with a respect for the natural character and beauty inherent in wood.

Describe when you first truly realized that you had artistic skills, and how you worked to develop those skills.

The starting point of my craft or artistic work may have been in fifth or sixth grade when my art teacher submitted one of my drawings to a citywide elementary school display at the Albright Art Gallery. About this time I started making airplane models and other simple wood projects. When I was in seventh or eighth grade my father made me a workbench which I still have.

I did not take any art or shop classes in high school when I concentrated on math, science and mechanical drawing because I planned to become an engineer. World War II ended during my senior year and since the military draft was still in effect, I entered Buffalo State Teachers' College while I waited to be drafted into the military.

At "Buff State" I entered the industrial arts program. Of all the classes, wood and metal shop interested me the most, especially wood shop. I also took several Art Department electives: drawing, jewelry making and ceramics. At this time I acquired a fine small camera, eventually working on photographic composition. These were all activities I thoroughly enjoyed.

Shortly after graduation, I entered the U.S. Air Force and attended the Aerial Photo Officer School, learning many highly skilled aerial and ground photo techniques. Eventually, I became an aerial photographer and, in my off time, took many still photographs related to my Air Force work. Some of my photos are in the Strategic Air and Space Museum.

When I was released from active military duty I returned to Buffalo and taught industrial arts woodworking; I stressed design. At home — I was married by then — I started building furniture. I purchased an old lathe and started woodturning and building smaller items such as jewelry boxes. Eventually, I joined the Western New York Woodturners where I really learned woodturning skills. These allowed for more creative expression in my work by teaching me how to explore the changes in grain pattern and colors which can change with the different locations within the same tree.

When I have a specific project planned I try to obtain wood with grain and color patterns that enhance the visual appearance of the finished piece. As I work on a turning, often the natural structure of the wood will determine its shape.

About thirty years ago I developed a strong interest in the Arts and Crafts Movement of the late 1800s to the early 1900s, particularly the furniture and ceramics. When our son purchased an Arts and Crafts bungalow in Houston, Texas, I started building furniture and accessories for him and his family.

The ceramics of the period gave me many design ideas for my woodturned projects. I have been fortunate enough to be the recipient of local and national honors.

What is your attraction to the Roycroft arts community and RALA? How has it impacted you as an artist?

In December of 2003 my wife and I attended the Roycroft Winter Show and I realized that the furniture and woodturned projects I made fit perfectly with those of the Roycroft Artisans. I applied, submitted photos and examples of my work to be juried and was accepted as a Roycroft Artisan.

When I discovered that an artisan was expected to participate in at least one show a year and to be juried annually in order to show development of my craft, I felt that this was beyond my capabilities. After all, I was 75 at the time. I discussed my concerns with Dorothy Markert, who was co-chairman of the artisan jury. She strongly encouraged me to participate, suggesting that I start with just a few items for a show. I became a Roycroft Artisan in 2004.

Participating in that first and in succeeding shows was one of the most satisfying and rewarding experiences of my life. People I had never met were admiring my works; some actually purchased them. In succeeding years, some people returned to see what new items I had made.

The annual jurying process made me look for new horizons in my woodturning. I began adding carved surface designs based on nature and Arts and Crafts ceramics. In 2007 I was awarded Master Artisan status.

Please share something else related to your craft which was not on this list of questions.

Recently, I had to reduce my woodworking and I no longer make enough items for a show although I am exploring designs based on the concept of SOFA — Sculptured Object, Functional Art.

Presently, I am concentrating on designing and making projects for present and future family, especially those who are now in high school and college.

Occasionally, I may be able to take on a request from outside the family.

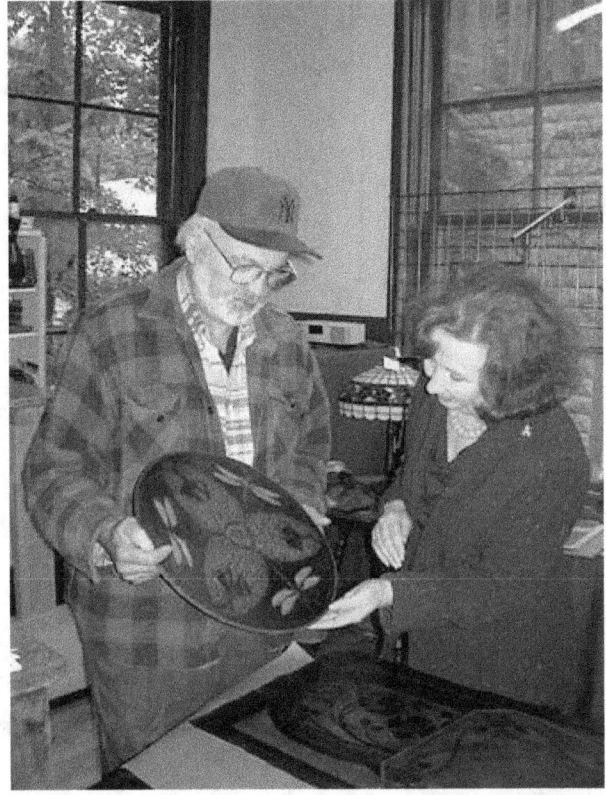

Describe your artistic specialty, and what you typically like to create.

I was inspired in my early childhood after seeing a leather wallet that was hand-tooled with a deer on it. I thought, "I want to do that." I purchased a hand-tooling kit and began my hobby of making my own wallet. That led me to become a member of the Niagara Frontier Craftsman.

What is your attraction to the Roycroft arts community and the Roycrofters-At-Large Association? How has it impacted you as an artist?

In early 1980 I began doing mall shows displaying and selling my work. During that time I met with Ted Candrowski of Tadora Leather Goods. Ted was retiring and selling his clicker press and dyes, which I then purchased. At the same time I was introduced to Kitty Turgeon, then owner of the Roycroft Gift Shop. I began reading books on the history and the founder of the Roycroft, Elbert Hubbard. Elbert's philosophy rang true to me with his inspirational sayings such as "Blessed is the man who has found his work" and "Head, heart and hand."

I was particularly fascinated with the Roycroft leather workers and the labor-intensive process of leather tooling. Seeing the original fine leather tooling was fascinating. I began crafting my own table mats, desk blotters, belts, key fobs and handbags. Lots and lots of handbags, all with the likeness philosophy of the Roycroft. I then realized my hobby had become my full-time career. In 1992 I was juried in to become a Roycroft craftsman, and in 2000 I was elevated to Roycroft Master Artisan, which I humbly accepted.

Where can people see and/or purchase your art?

In 1995 I rented space in the Furniture Building of the Roycroft Campus giving demonstrations of my craft, and I continued selling my work. It was quite a journey from selling and displaying my work at mall shows. It felt like home. I became very close to Onda and Chester Dylewski, the owners of Roycroft Antiques on the campus. I also began selling my work to Dard Hunter III, who traveled to the annual Grove Park Inn Mission Show in Asheville, North Carolina, and began sending my handbags to them for sale.

After the passing of Chester and Onda I concentrated mainly on my home studio, and travel wasn't as necessary. I was comfortable selling to online customers through my website, GallowayLeather.com, which I am now updating. I am still actively selling my work throughout the campus, Dard Hunter III, Gallery of the Mountains at Grove Park, and to friends and family who are always asking for coin purses, bookmarks and key fobs.

As an artist, what has been your most significant achievement, or proudest moment, to date?

What I'm most proud of is my creation of my table mats. Professor Stanley Matthews of Hobart William Smith College purchased my dragonfly/gingko leaf table mat that the college gifted to the Tanaka Foundation in Japan for display at the Tanaka Museum. And, for the recognition of my work in publications such as Grove Park Inn Arts & Crafts Furniture by Bruce Johnston, Artistic Leather of the Arts and Crafts Era by Daniel Lees and Style 1900 Magazine.

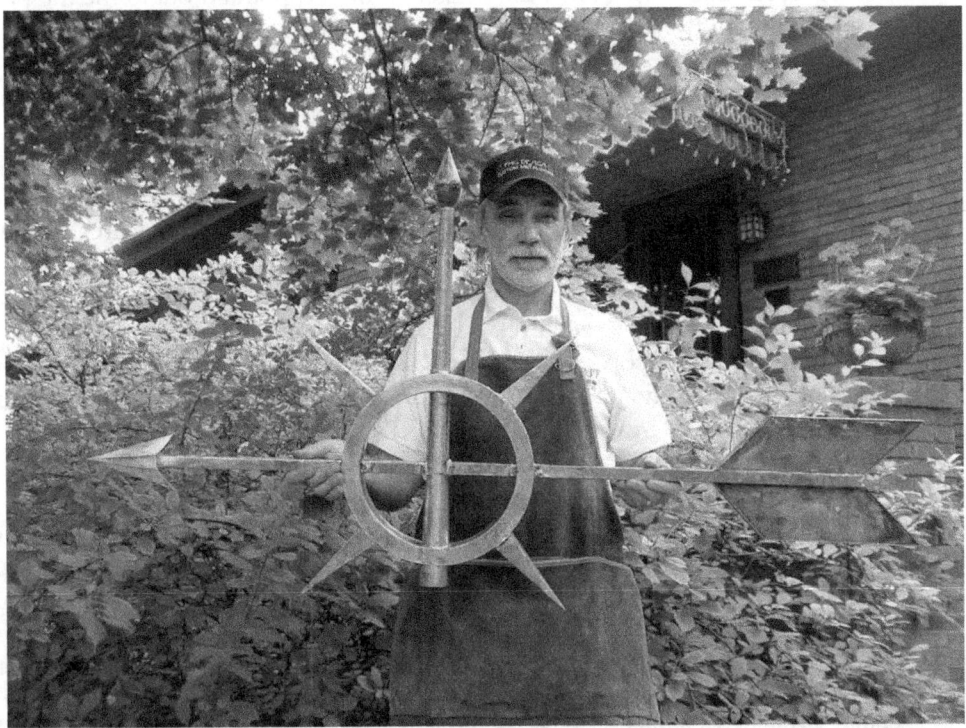

Describe your artistic specialty and what you typically like to create.

I work on metalsmithing, mostly copper, and my particular specialty is "repoussé." I taught for several years on the Roycroft Campus when they began the classes program — had beginner classes in April and intermediate classes in October. I now teach in Chicago and Asheville, North Carolina.

Describe when you first truly realized that you had artistic skills, and how you worked to develop those skills.

I loved art since I was a kid growing up in Buffalo, and I received all sorts of scholarships to attend Buffalo State and Albright-Knox art classes while in high school. I graduated high school with the largest scholarship — fully paid tuition at the Columbus School of Art and Design. After finishing freshman year I left to attend The School of the Art Institute of Chicago.

Who/what are your inspirations, and why?

I'm inspired by everything around me, especially nature. For example, when my wife Anastasia and I traveled to the Pacific Northwest, I saw the magnificent tall cypress trees on an island rainforest in Washington State and I was inspired to create all sorts of tree designs — whether hanging on a slope or many trees in a group. We also became TreeKeepers in Chicago, taking care of city and parks trees as trained volunteers. We had tree experts in their field teach us about the diseases, how to plant them, how and when to prune and so much more. Now I create designs of flowers, gingko leaves, maples with seedheads, and oak and such.

From copper I've made large- and small-size koi fish and bunny rabbits, tiny birds, ravens, seahorses and water lilies. I do my own designs and interpretations of what I see. Anastasia, as a longtime master gardener, pointed out to me the prairie flowers of the midwest and the benefits of their "no extra watering needed," which opened my eyes more.

I also do my research into old Arts and Crafts work and create designs of my own version of work.

Describe the space where you typically create, and what is so special about that place?

My studio workspace is several rooms I opened up into a huge area where I have machinery for woodworking, all metalworking equipment, and kick press and photography tools too, all in the lower level of our home. It's not a basement since the house is higher than street level.

We live in a large corner 90-year-old historic Chicago bungalow and I use the lower level as my studio and workshop. It's very convenient since I can work any time of day and night.

Sometimes, when the weather is warm, I sit and beat copper on our front porch. Families walking by to the nearby park, especially children, want to know what I'm doing. When they see the final result they are amazed that this can be done from just a plain piece of copper with small hand tools I've created.

Our neighborhood is registered as a National and Chicago Historic Bungalow District, and living across from 90-plus-year-old Arts and Crafts-designed homes is very inspiring. The last two years I restored the front walk up to our steps and the metal and stained glass marquee overhang to our front entry door. Chicago's former Mayor (Richard) Daley was given an award by American Bungalow Magazine in 2001 for creating the Historic Chicago Bungalow Association to save the bungalows. This year we won the Richard Driehaus Foundation's first prize for the marquee project. Now it will last another 90 years for future generations to enjoy.

Do you travel from show to show? What are the best and worst aspects of life on the road? Feel free to share your most memorable story.

We drive a packed rental van to each show and I participate in four shows a year with my wife Anastasia. I have done it alone, but it's not as much fun!

Starting in February with the annual Arts and Crafts Conference at the Grove Park Inn in Asheville, North Carolina, we next travel in May to the Arts and Crafts Chicago show in the nearby River Forest/Oak Park area during the "Wright Plus" weekend. At the end of June, as a Roycrofter I participate at the annual Roycrofters-At-Large Association's Summer Festival in East Aurora, New York. My last show, in September, is the Twin Cities Show in Minneapolis/St. Paul, where many Arts and Crafts bungalow enthusiasts live.

Anastasia's role in my art creativity is central since she organizes and does all the office work, paperwork and bookkeeping, leaving me free to beat the metal. We are a team and always travel together. She keeps timetables for my workshops so they flow smoothly, from projects to lists, evaluation sheets, materials and details as needed.

Anastasia tried beating copper during my very first workshop at the Roycroft Copper Shop and by 11 a.m. she gave it up, never to touch the tools again! She has great admiration for everyone who take my workshops, doing copper repoussé for hours, and tells them so.

What are the best and worst aspects of life on the road? The best is Anastasia's tasty snacks, treats and delicious Greek food; our discussions about all sorts of things; the music we love and getting to the shows safe! Also, meeting and catching up with our friends and fellow artisans at the shows is another highlight.

The worst aspect is interstate highway safety! This year, going to Asheville, the icy conditions and snow as in past years was no fun. Southerners don't know how to drive in bad conditions; they speed instead of going slowly!

Another one a few years ago was returning in April from East Aurora, New York, after the Roycroft jury, and we were almost killed on the interstate in Ohio. A small truck hauling equipment lost one of it's tires, heading straight for our rental sedan at 80-plus miles an hour! Luckily, the tire crossed our path and went into the farm fields, otherwise the 18-wheeler behind us and SUVs next to us would have all piled together on top of us.

Anastasia and I have had a few memorable stories, and here are a couple.

The year 2015 was very memorable at the Grove Park Inn because I had the chance to use Dirk Van Erp's 100-plus-year-old tools. The Dirk Van Erp Foundation invited me several times to come and beat a copper bowl. It was a highlight of this year's Arts and Crafts Conference. Van Erp's lamps at recent auctions go for $50,000-plus prices.

Another memorable moment occurred in 2008 at my beginner's copper workshop at the Roycroft Campus. I had a *New York Times* reporter taking the class. Nobody knew this until Anastasia was collecting the evaluation forms at the end and the reporter said she didn't have to turn one in. Everyone looked at her and after that she told us she was writing a story about the workshop and took video on her cellphone which you can see on the web. Laura M. Holson wrote, "I will never complain about paying $200 for a handcrafted copper bowl again." It was a very positive story and a big surprise to be written up in the *New York Times*!

What is your attraction to the Roycroft arts community and the Roycrofters-At-Large Association? How has it impacted you as an artist?

I was first told about the Roycrofter Renaissance in 1995 by Kathleen West and Janice McDuffy when we were a group of seven artisans invited to the first Craftsman Farms Symposium in New Jersey. Kathleen and Janice made sure I would apply at the next Roycroft jury, especially since I grew up in Buffalo.

I like the utopian community ideas — to work and produce beautiful handmade things. I live in Chicago and produce all my work there, which is another center of the Arts and Crafts Movement with many examples of great architecture in homes, commercial buildings, parks and art.

As an artist, I like to create my own copper designs in the Arts and Crafts style, for the 21st century and beyond. I also like being with the Roycrofters and participating in the annual jury adding my knowledge and expertise in classic art and seeing new artisans creating beautiful objects.

I see fellow Roycroft artisans' work at the Grove Park Inn, then at the organization's shows and the Chautauqua show we all did. I greatly enjoy their maturity and creative works. Chicago is not close to the Roycroft Campus and meeting other Roycrofters is a great experience. Everyone does beautiful work and the creativity is wonderful!

Where can people see and/or purchase your art?

All my work is done by me only, therefore it takes time to design, create and make each item. I have samples for people to look at and order when they come to my exhibition shows and when I teach the copper workshops.

My website has samples of my work, but I do not update it much anymore.

Clients find me — they Google my name and see my work images online. People have posted my work — from a letter opener to mailboxes, numbers and more. When they buy a FMG-designed item, they're buying "made by Frank Glapa only."

I sell only at the Roycroft Copper Shop in East Aurora.

Recently I was able to buy back one of my first (#016) copper bungalow mailboxes made before I became a Roycrofter. Here's what the seller from California emailed me: *Hi Frank. I'm so glad to hear it came back to you! I hated to sell it, but it had been staring me in the face for almost five years. I really commend your craftsmanship. The first thing I said to the buyers of our bungalow was, 'The mailbox does not stay.' I am trying to remember where I bought it. I think it was out of the Roycroft catalog? I am so glad it will find a good home, but I will miss it. Regards, Jennifer Auslund*

As an artist, what is the best piece of advice that you were ever given? What words of inspiration or advice would you offer those who might aspire to follow in your artistic footsteps?

Former Roycroft Master in metal, now deceased, Rich Reitz told me, "Frank, you can beat this metal," which I didn't do. That was the best idea ever! I started to beat the copper and kept on going until I realized using small hand tools I was forming for my own use were a better ergonomic design than the large hammers. My hands never tired and I could keep on beating copper.

I now tell all my students, "Copper is very forgiving and you can fix your mistakes." Hopefully one of them can make it even better. As one of the Roycrofters told me, "I'm training the competition." I sure hope so, because there was nobody to train me when I started.

When someone looks at something you have created, what type of reaction or emotion do you hope to see, and why?

People always want to touch my work, which I like for them to do. Copper repoussé is a very tactile material and they get drawn to it. I love the fact that they touch my pieces because I get a nice patina from their handling. They are amazed that all this work — whether it's a chiming clock, boxes with sliding tops, birds, fish, animals, letters, numbers and more — all started with a flat piece of copper metal.

Do you have an artistic goal — a bucket list project — that hasn't yet been met?

My artistic goal is to pass on the art of copper repoussé to everyone wanting to learn it. When I began doing the copper, nobody was around I could ask. One Roycrofter, Rich Reitz at Craftsman Farms, gave me some pointers that I can beat the copper. So having art training from the Art Institute of Chicago I kept at it and finally made my wife copper earrings from small cutoffs. She liked them and I was on my way making jewelry. I can do all sorts of art on copper, it just takes time and patience since I do all the work myself.

You never know what is next on the art horizon of my mind. Last year I created a huge and heavy fireplace screen with doors and ginkgo leaf repoussé designs in the front corners. My work is limitless, it just takes time to make it happen because I can't grow two more hands, as Anastasia likes to remind me.

As an artist, what has been your most significant achievement, or proudest moment, to date?

In 2012 I was invited to have my work exhibited along with a few other Roycroft Masters in the new Burchfield Penney Art Center in their Margaret L. Wendt and R. William Doolittle galleries, mixed in with their Arts and Crafts antiques collection. The Well Crafted: Roycroft Then and Now exhibit was so popular they extended it for a few more months. It was such an honor to have my mantel clock displayed above Charles Rolfs' carved living room settee and other such luminaries of 100 years ago. My large pinecone box and rose bowl sitting next to Karl Kipp's bud flower vase in the display cabinet — they looked like they were made from back then.

I just wished my parents were alive for the opening reception to see my artwork displayed in a 21st century museum across from Albright-Knox Art Gallery. What a dream!

Please share something else related to your craft which was not on this list of questions.

In Chicago we speak by invitation in neighborhood grammar schools about art during Career Day. We talk to fourth graders and up about creating and making art and how you can make a living doing something you love! We tell them, "You will have fun and stay happy doing what you love — just don't expect to be millionaires." We also show them how the art is done and that if you have happiness, that's a very important part of living, not just money!

The young students understand it, and usually the next time they show up dressed in painters' smocks, with the girls sticking paintbrushes in their hair as adornment. We loved it — they got it!

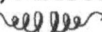
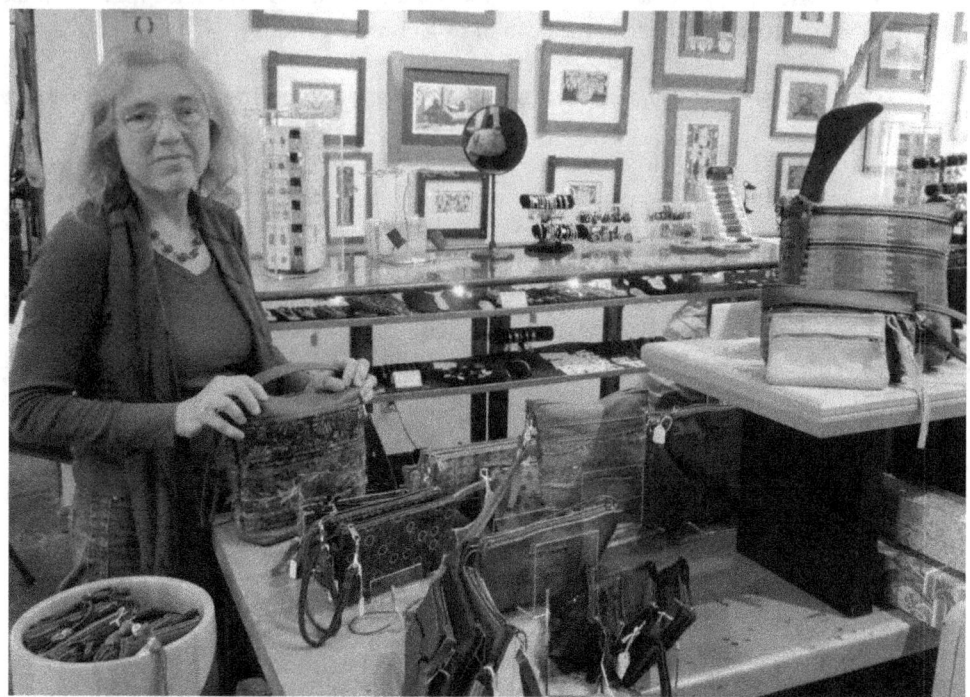

Describe your artistic specialty and what you typically like to create.

My specialty is soft, fabric-like garment leather. I cut and sew it a lot like you do with fabric, except leather is not square and it has thick and thin spots and different grain from one end to the other. Each pattern piece is laid out individually.

I make handbags and accessories, mostly — but not all — for women.

What I really love to do is work with bright, jewel-tone colors, and to combine them with other fibers like handprinted wool, handprinted quilt fabrics, tapestry and hand-spun yarn. And beads, too. I think of myself as a fiber artist who happens to use a lot of leather.

Describe when you first truly realized that you had artistic skills, and how you worked to develop those skills.

I always loved to draw. When I was in grade school I found what they were teaching to be pretty monotonous. Our desks were designed so you could secretly draw while you appeared to pay attention, and so I did! I was very dismayed when on a day I was absent, they had "desk clean-out day." Mine was packed full of old drawings.

During a sleepover at my cousin Jill's house when I was 14, she showed me how to paint with oils. From that moment I knew I wanted to be a famous artist.

I fell in love with the brilliant colors and the mood evoked by Impressionist painters, and tried to imitate their style. What interested me most was painting nature. Being outside — or near a window if inside — was important to me going back to my earliest memories, and I wanted to capture the exquisite beauty of nature that I saw all around me at different times of day and during different seasons — maybe not winter so much.

I graduated from high school in 1970 with a partial scholarship to RIT. But with the wisdom of a 17-year-old, I decided that I'd had enough of school and would become a famous Impressionist on my own. When my friends went off to college, I looked for an art-related job to make money whilst I worked on my art. I found a job as a seamstress in a hippie leather shop.

I had no idea how to sew leather, though I had taught myself to sew. No one else who owned a leather shop in Rochester, New York — there were about eight of them — knew how to sew either! Most of them made some pretty awful stuff, but people wanted leather then and bought it anyhow. I was determined to only make really beautiful, artistic stuff, correctly sewn.

To everyone's surprise, I had an amazing talent for creating leather goods. I appliquéd and fringed and beaded and completely made up how to do it as I went along. It was a very creative process and I had so many ideas of things I wanted to make that my painting dream got put on a back burner.

I met my future husband that year and a year later, when I was 18, we opened our own store.

I learned that I had to make things that didn't always excite me to please our customers. And, I had to make a lot of stuff to fill a store all by myself. Sometimes creativity took a back seat to making sales and just to making stuff quickly.

The store only lived two years, but then in 1973 we did our first craft show. It was fantastic and it looked like a marvelous way to be an almost-artist and make a living. Craft shows were hot and crafts were being re-discovered again. People came in masses and there were times we almost sold out. It was an exciting time and we felt we were part of a movement to bring handmade back into peoples' lives and fill their homes with made-by-hand objects.

As I continued to respond to what customers wanted to buy, my work lost its creative spark. It sold as fast as I made it, but it did not please me for many years. My work turned into my job and my creativity went into my fiber arts pastimes — knitting, spinning and hooking rugs — and my garden.

In 2001, I was meditating while watching the sun rise over Chautauqua Lake when I suddenly heard a voice say, "If you don't like what you make, why don't you try making what you do like?"

I replied, in my head, "Because I don't think it will sell."

Replied the voice, "How do you know? You've never tried it!"

So I thought, "Wow, that's true. I ought to try that."

And suddenly, dozens of new designs in bright, delicious colors poured into my head, complete with measurements and how-to instructions for assembling them. I could hardly wait to get home and start creating. That morning completely changed my life.

New ideas continued to come, and making my new work made me want to go into the studio every morning. My work began to resemble those paintings I never had time to paint, especially when I began to combine my beloved fiber arts with the leather.

My work became something no one else does — the combinations look to me like Impressionist paintings — and I finally feel like the artist I always wanted to be!

Describe the space where you typically create, and what is so special about that place?

Since my first memories I always loved to be outside, or, if inside, always near a window. I was endlessly fascinated by fireflies when I was only five. School was hard for me because we were stuck inside all day and I felt like like a prisoner. I would come home from school and go out into the woods alone for hours at a time just to wander or sit in my favorite spots. In high school I read book after book on Eastern religions, and also found John Muir. They were so similar. My time in the woods usually inspired me to paint. I also spent hours looking at the moon from my bedroom window — a mystic I was but no one to share it with!

Buying a house in the country was my dream, and in 1976 we moved south of 5 & 20 to Yates County. It was real country. It was wild. The stars come down into the tree branches, not just the top of the sky like in the city! Coyotes howl, bears walk through and the wind blows hard. It is quiet and there is peace that is alive in the air. Very sweet air.

This all becomes part of my work. In my three country houses, the biggest room became my studio. It either had big windows or they were added. Sunlight and breezes and the sounds of birds and animals pour through. I feel it surround me all day as I work, and I take frequent breaks to step outside for a deeper immersion. The sky changes colors and the wind changes directions and that all goes into my work. There is two feet of snow? Oh, goodie. I don't have to go anywhere so I'll just make more stuff!

Each of my houses, starting with my childhood home, was on a hilltop with a long-distance view. There is magic out there in the distant horizon, and I watch it all day long until the sun sets behind it. And later, the moon follows. That goes into my work, too.

When I am alone working, I'm not alone. I'm surrounded by countless living beings, and that also goes into my work.

I enjoy what I do and I enjoy where I live and work.

Do you travel from show to show? What are the best and worst aspects of life on the road? Feel free to share your most memorable story.

I leave home 15 times a year for craft shows, and they are still exciting even after all this time. It's a chance to see all my work on display together, like a giant painting. And I meet all sorts of interesting people and visit with artist friends I've known since 1973.

This year all my shows but one are local — Rochester, Buffalo and the Finger Lakes. Local is a few hundred miles to me. I'm happy not to drive eight hours like I used to. That was hard when I had a family at home, and I don't need to prove that I can drive like a trucker anymore. I can. So what?

Where can people see and/or purchase your art?

The Copper Shop in East Aurora, New York, and the Handwork Cooperative Craft Store in Ithaca, New York.

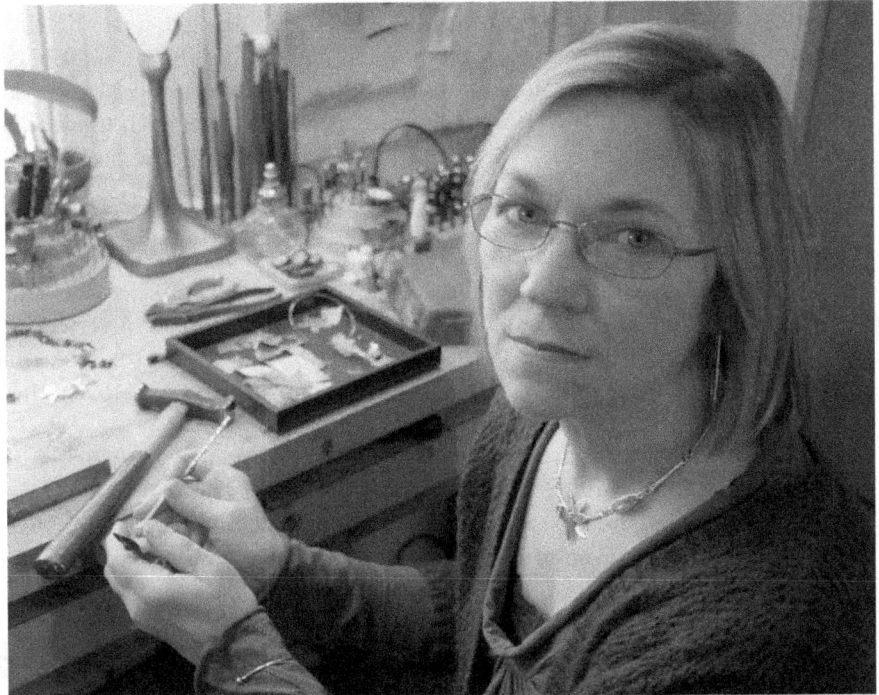

Describe your artistic specialty and what you typically like to create.

For the last 15 years I have been exploring working with precious metals to design and make handcrafted, one-of-a-kind jewelry which also incorporate semi-precious gems and pearls.

I like designing but my favorite part is directly working with metal-forging, forming and fabricating, along with weaving and crocheting silver and gold wire. It is in those moments that I feel the plasticity of the metal. As I am working, I can see my ideas take shape, from raw metal to a shape that will take on a life of its own.

Previously, I studied and was trained as a printmaker and spent about 25 years creating, producing and showing my etchings and wood cuts in various regional galleries and institutions. After a long time I found myself wanting to work in a smaller scale and a more intimate way to express my ideas, images and designs. Working with precious metals and gemstones in a direct manner to make jewelry pieces provided me with that direction and opportunity.

Who/what are your inspirations, and why?

Life and the natural world that I am surrounded by have had a great influence on what I make — the flora and fauna that I see outside my studio and home, the people I encounter, the countries and cultures that I have lived in and visited.

My father was in the military, and when I was a child we lived in and traveled to many locations around the world and in this country. Because of this I was exposed to and immersed in the cultures of each place we lived, many of which had very strong folk art and craft traditions. It had a great influence on me as to how I viewed the world and how the expression of arts and crafts fit into our daily lives.

During many of the transfers to a new location we would stay with my grandmother for prolonged visits. She was deeply involved in arts and crafts, working in a variety of media. She taught me weaving, ceramics, leather tooling, quilting and painting from the time I was a young girl. Her home was like a wonderful craft center where you were encouraged to explore and "play" with different materials and to never be afraid to try something new. She also was a naturalist who exposed me to and taught me about plants, birds and animals while on walks in the woods. She taught me to have respect and awe for the world we live in. She has been the greatest role model and inspiration in my life as a person and as an artist.

Describe the space where you typically create, and what is so special about that place?

I have a lovely studio in my home that is divided into three areas for different aspects of my work. My design and final finishing area is in a converted bedroom that has a northern exposure, thus flooding my studio with wonderful light. It also looks out onto Tonawanda Creek where I can look up from my work to see the water and the abundance of birds flying around.

The two other areas are set up in my basement and garage, which are more practical for working on the heavy forging, polishing, grinding and etching of my work — the messy part of creating jewelry. It is truly wonderful that I have a space that I can easily work in at any given time without having to go to another space to create ... and at the same time be surrounded by a lot of inspiration.

What is your attraction to the Roycroft arts community and the Roycrofters-At-Large Association? How has it impacted you as an artist?

Prior to moving to Western New York my exposure was through art history classes featuring Frank Lloyd Wright's beautiful buildings, which incorporated many details and features highlighting the crafts to complete his vision of a home. At the same time I was studying printmaking and became interested with the history and tradition of guilds within my field.

When I transitioned from creating etchings and woodcuts to working in metal to create jewelry, I found a community of artists that were following the ideals of the original Roycroft Artisans, with high standards of design and craftsmanship. I became involved with showing my work at shows with the Roycrofters-At-Large Association, and then I became a Roycroft Artisan and then a Master Artisan. As an artist, it has been a very meaningful to be part of a community of artists that strive to keep handcrafted arts of the highest standards alive.

Being part of this community has encouraged and motivated me to keep learning and improving the quality of my work.

As an artist, what is the best piece of advice that you were ever given? What words of inspiration or advice would you offer those who might aspire to follow in your artistic footsteps?

As an artist and craftsman I do get approached by people interested in "doing what I do" because they want to learn how do "it" too. Quite often they have a hard time defining what "it" is, but I respect that they are responding on some visceral level to my work so I tend to ask them a series of questions:
- What exactly do you want to make?
- Why do you want to make jewelry or work with metals?

• Then, I ask them to reflect on what appeals to them about the notion of making and working with metal and gemstones.

• Finally, I ask them if they have done anything to pursue their desire.

I encourage them to take a class, read, research and look at tutorials online, and then to jump in and do it and not wait for the right moment, and not to be afraid of trying and failing or making mistakes. And, I tell them to practice and become passionate about what they want to create.

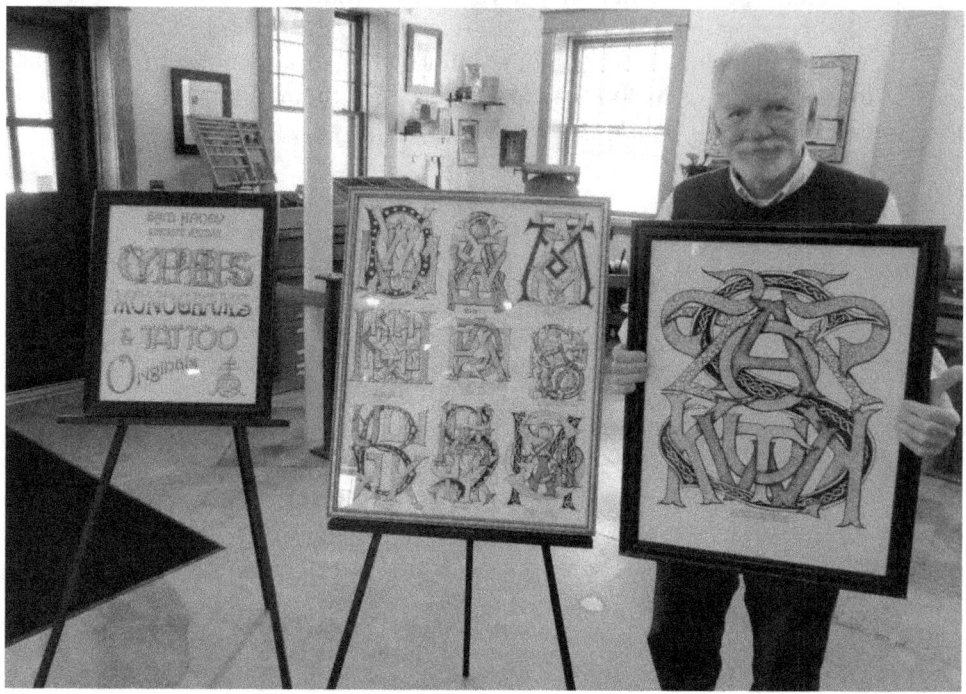

Describe your artistic specialty and what you typically like to create.

Pen and ink! My favorite medium!

Describe when you first truly realized that you had artistic skills, and how you worked to develop those skills.

I became interested in drawing, sketching and doodling at an early age. My first place award-winning pen and ink drawing was a statewide contest of junior high school students. My parents drove me to the awards ceremony in Williamsport, Pennsylvania, over 100 miles away. The gold lapel pin they presented to me is one of my favorite possessions. That day marked the beginning of my interest in artwork. My woeful high school grades were the result of my doodling and sketching instead of learning the "three Rs."

As the years passed I became more aware of the unlimited application for pen and ink work. I tried other mediums like oil, acrylic, watercolors and pastels, but I decided to concentrate on pen and ink. My collection of Bibles, old etchings and engravings have provided me a source of reference for my monograms and cyphers.

Monograms are usually three letters that include a person's first, middle and last names. The most well-known monograms might be JFK.

Cyphers (Si Far), a variant of cipher, may include a secret or encoded message that may be deciphered by the recipient.

My favorite passion is the creation of a cypher or decorative intertwined spelling of a family name. The challenge is to create artwork with the discipline of making all the letters fit. The cypher should be balanced with light and dark space between the entwining letters. The longer the name, the more letters and the more challenging and time-consuming it is to encypher. (I use more erasers than pencils ... just kidding).

The first initial letter of the family's name is usually the more dominant. The other letters may be in any order — reversed, turned upside down or backwards. The challenge is to create a cypher that appears balanced between light and dark and well spaced.

Describe the space where you typically create, and what is so special about that place?

My studio is in the basement of an 1850's farmhouse, where my drawing board shares the small space with the furnace, a hot water tank, miscellaneous shelves and a few mice. Fortunately it's cool in the summer and warm in the winter! Although some visitors don't appreciate the clutter, I know where everything is.

What is your attraction to the Roycroft arts community and the Roycrofters-At-Large Association? How has it impacted you as an artist?

I've always considered that as a self-taught amateur artist, my portfolio of illustrations could never earn enough to support my future plans. While employed, I exhibited my art at local art and craft shows. Friends, neighbors and customers suggested I take some art classes. They also suggested I apply for membership in the Roycrofters-At-Large Association — so I submitted examples of my work to a jury of members and was accepted into the organization. Since new members are juried annually to determine if the artisan has improved in quality, I am aware I must continually strive to do even better each time I go back to the drawing board.

As an artist, what is the best piece of advice that you were ever given? What words of inspiration or advice would you offer those who might aspire to follow in your artistic footsteps?

The best advice that was ever given to me was from my mother. When she bought me a coloring book and crayons she told me, "Don't go over the lines." My advice to artists today is, "Go over the lines — and be creative!"

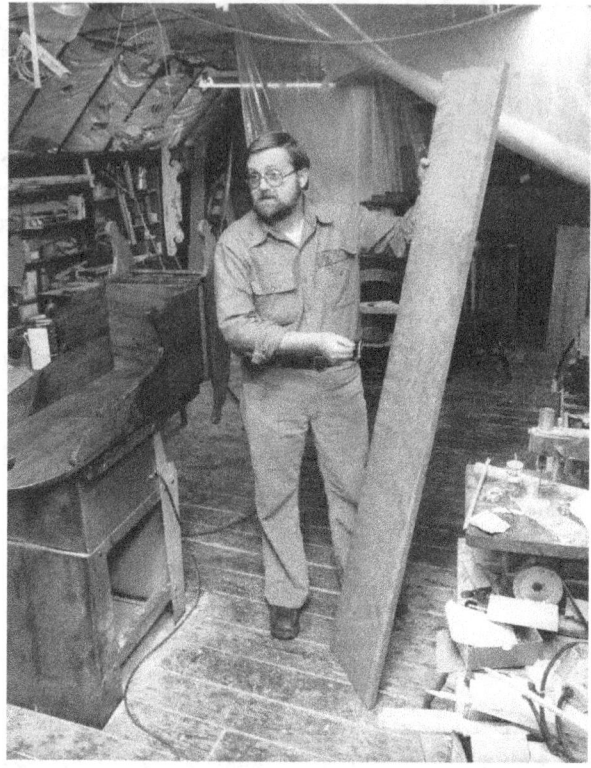

Describe your artistic specialty and what you typically like to create.

I am a woodpecker, mostly making furniture.

Describe the space where you typically create, and what is so special about that place?

My workspace is a 28 x 48 shop with great natural light. It is located behind an 1850 schoolhouse that once was my workshop and now serves as a showroom.

Where can people see and/or purchase your art?

My work can be seen and purchased at the Schoolhouse Gallery, located at 1054 Olean Road, East Aurora, New York.

As an artist, what has been your most significant achievement, or proudest moment, to date?

My most significant work, along with my partner Ben Little, was the work that we did at City Honors High School. We did 22 library tables, all the computer desks and the librarian's main checkout desk. We also did the main office standup reception desk complete with files and drawers and a free-standing 36-inch high cabinet with four double file drawers, all made of quarter-sawn white oak in the Arts and Crafts style.

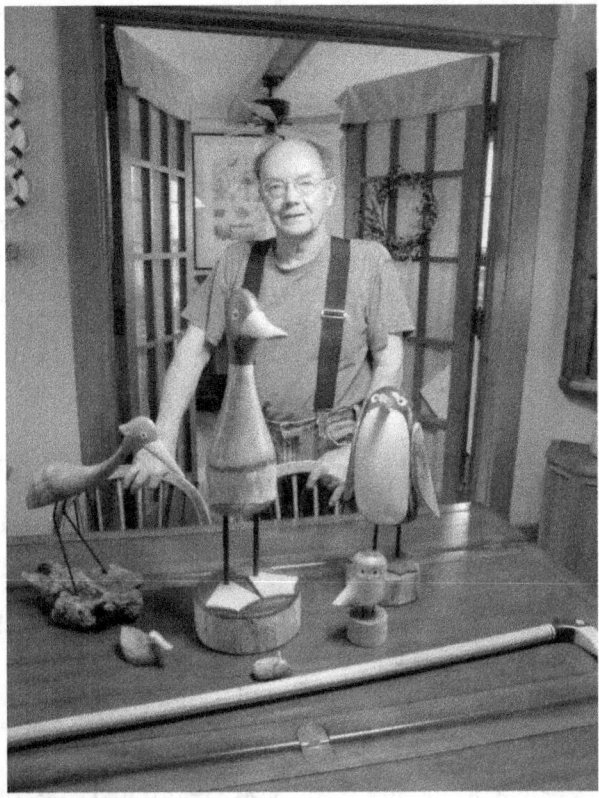

Describe your artistic specialty and what you typically like to create.

I'm a Roycroft Master Artisan in wood sculpture, and I've always had to be working with my hands. I've had no formal art training or schooling, just a couple of classes as part of my occupational therapy course back in college. Just taking raw materials and making something pretty or beautiful from it has always appealed to me.

For the most part I specialize in animal sculptures such as geese, penguins, herons, owls, ducks, fish and other creations of varying sizes. The flying duck sculptures are among my favorites. Each one is different because I use tree stumps that have projections that look like feathers when finished. I can make them in a range of sizes, too. I make everything from little wooden mice measuring just an inch or two to birds and fish stretching approximately three feet in length.

Describe when you first truly realized that you had artistic skills, and how you worked to develop those skills.

While my professional career included 20 years of service to the United States Air Force as an occupational therapist, I loved working with wood and with my hands from a very early age. As a Boy Scout back in 1957, I earned second place in a whittling contest sponsored by Boys' Life magazine. Working with wood is both a hobby and a release for my creativity, and it has lasted a lifetime.

I've always had my hobbies. When I was in the Boy Scouts I used to whittle neckerchief slides. I also liked to build models, and I remember going up to the hobby shop when I was a boy and getting model cars and boats and that sort of thing.

When college called, I decided to attend the University of Buffalo to study occupational therapy. At that time we learned to use arts and crafts as a treatment for people with disabilities and injuries. I was pretty good with my hands and I started to build special splints and prostheses for people with arm and hand injuries. A lot of ingenuity and creativity were required in my job.

When I retired from the Air Force, I decided to go off on my own and do something with my hands, and I began making wooden toys. We lived then near a lake in Texas and when I would go to craft shows I would see these people using driftwood, and I thought why not try that? So I began making toys and figures and gradually got more into sculpture. I like to use Texas cedar driftwood, but since moving up here I use a lot more of the northern driftwoods from Lake Erie. This part of Lake Erie is perfect because the winds blow the driftwood to this end.

What is your attraction to the Roycroft arts community and the Roycrofters-At-Large Association? How has it impacted you as an artist?

I knew little or nothing about the Roycroft community when we moved to East Aurora 20 years ago to be closer to my father. I didn't even know there was a history of that here. I just thought it was a nice little town and a nice place to live. Only after we lived here awhile did I find out about the Roycrofters. I've been doing two craft show a year for 20 years in East Aurora and that's how I got to know some of the Roycroft people and decided to join them.

Where can people see and/or purchase your art?

My work can be found in five gift stores — two in Texas, one in the Thousand Islands and two in East Aurora ... The Copper Shop on the Roycroft Campus and The Schoolhouse Gallery on Olean Road. I also participate in six or seven nearby art shows each year, including the Syracuse Arts & Crafts Festival, Letchworth Arts & Crafts Show, Chautauqua Arts & Crafts Festival, Allentown Art Festival, Rochester Clothesline Art Festival and the Hammondsport Festival of Crafts. Nowadays we pretty much stay close to home.

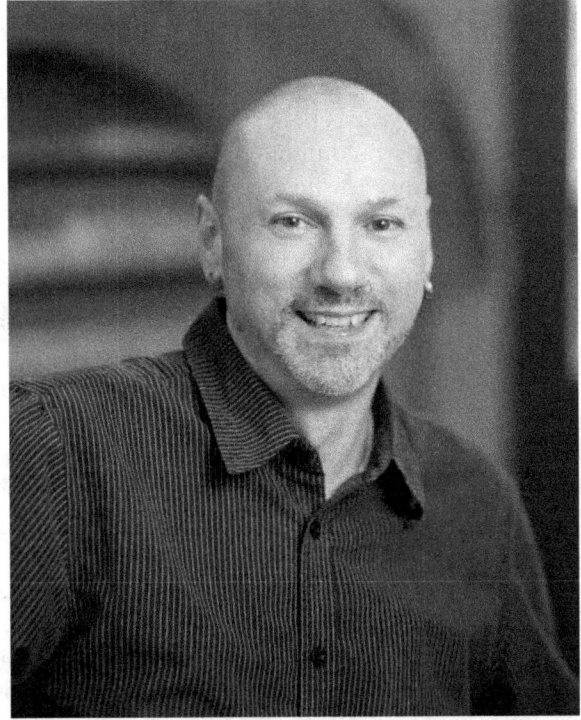

Describe your artistic specialty and what you typically like to create.

My artistic specialty as a Roycroft Renaissance Master Artisan is painting. Although, visually, my oeuvre is eclectic, the kind of work I typically like to create is the sort that has deeper meaning than what is seen on the surface. I like to imbed my art with symbols and iconography that gives viewers the opportunity to experience the work on a heightened level.

For example, a landscape painting like "Among the Fallen," which is a painting of a fallen tree set in a mountainous landscape, can be understood as just that, a landscape with a fallen tree. But to look at it more deeply, it can be interpreted as an environmental statement, cautioning humankind of the dangers of deforestation and our impact on the environment. From another point of view it can be seen as a metaphor for the loss of life, or for change, and all of the pathos that comes with the great changes and upheavals that happen in our lives.

This sort of work continues the tradition of Symbolism, which was an art movement at the turn of the last century that spawned from the Romantic movement. The Arts and Crafts movement and the Roycroft community were also offspring of Romanticism, and my role as a Roycroft Artisan continues the Romantic tradition and interprets it for the conditions facing today's world.

Who/what are your inspirations, and why?

The artists who have inspired me are those who use their art as a vehicle to effect positive changes in the world. Contemporary artists that come to mind are Sue Coe, and my mentor Jim Davies who I studied with in college. These are artists whose work points to where things have gone awry in the modern world, and whose work, conversely, offers ideas and solutions for how to remedy the ills of a corrupt society.

Believing that art should have a purpose beyond the making of pretty pictures naturally attracts me to original rebel artists that were working at the turn of the last century and prior – artists like Dante Gabriel Rossetti, Gustav Klimt, Paul Gauguin and Wassily Kandinsky. The founder of the Arts and Crafts movement, William Morris, was such an artist. Morris believed that art, and the creation of a beautiful artistic living environment, would uplift people and bring about positive change in society. He also believed that artistic expression was good for the soul, and that to practice art was a way to foster contentment. These are the kind of artists that inspire me to create work that asks us to reevaluate our culture, our politics, our purpose in life, and what, ultimately, the meaning of life is.

I also cannot discount the strong influence traditional Japanese, and other Far Eastern art, has had on me. I have been studying Japanese art and culture since I was a teenager, and the values of the Japanese tea ceremony (Chanoyu), in particular, has left an indelible mark. The tea ceremony embraces all of the arts as a single unit: Painting, crafts (like pottery), flower arranging, calligraphy, poetry, fashion and architecture all combine to create one statement. The moral and spiritual values that encompass the tea ceremony are also precious to me.

Describe the space where you typically create, and what is so special about that place?

I would describe my studio space as very modest by most standards. I work from home and live in a 1913 American Foursquare, which was a popular style of middle-class home at the beginning of the last century. A foursquare is essentially comprised of four rooms downstairs and four rooms upstairs. My studio is located in one of the bedrooms upstairs and is only 11 x 14. I have a drafting table, a workbench and space for an easel. There is not a lot of room to move around, and I guess my preference of small, simple, and of avoiding the extravagant has something to do with the "Japanese" in me.

Traditionally, the Japanese composed rooms out of tatami mats. A tatami is composed of a 2:1 ratio and roughly measures 3 x 6 – this was considered all of the room a person needed to live. You can sit and work in this amount of space, you can prepare food and eat in this space, and it is room enough to lie down and sleep. I guess I believe that I don't need a lot of space. Outside of my paints and other art supplies, the room is lined with books, there is a chair for me to sit on, and there is a small stereo for music. In between these things, there's not much more room than a tatami mat.

I do have a corner in the basement set aside as a workshop for messy work. I build my own supports for my paintings, and this is where I cut and assemble the armatures and stretch my canvases. I often lay my grounds and prime the canvases in this space as well. Because of the size of my studio, I tend to work on a single piece at a time, creating relatively small works – very unlike other artists who tend to spread out a series of paintings and work on several at one time, or who work on a monumental scale.

Another bedroom in the home is used as my wife and business partner, Barbara Pierce's, office. The office is used to manage our architectural design and art business, CJ Hurley Century Arts.

The formal rooms of our home, the living room and dining room, showcase the hand-painted architectural friezes that I'm probably most known for in Arts and Crafts circles; these rooms act as a sort of showroom for this part of my work.

What is your attraction to the Roycroft arts community and the Roycrofters-At-Large Association? How has it impacted you as an artist?

My greatest attraction to the Roycroft arts community and the reason I wanted to join the Roycrofters-At-Large Association is for the group's dedication to hand-craftsmanship. For me, as our society becomes more and more mechanized and reliant on technology, hand-craftsmanship is the epitome of the arts. We are rapidly losing the skills required to do things with our own hands. Computers make it possible to "draw" perfectly straight and uniform lines, take a two-dimensional rendering and transform it into a three-dimensional one, and there is no longer a need to learn to paint when you can take a photograph and hit a button on your computer that makes it look like a painting.

But machined work is very cold, calculated and sterile. The imperfection inherent to the process of handcrafting is what brings a sense of humanity into the work being created. Even as one attempts mastery by uniting the mind and body while working, the fallible hand brings character to the created object. The imperfections truly are what make the artwork perfect.

The Roycrofters-At-Large Association has also helped to lift me from the oppression of the contemporary art scene's obsession with the "new." I think the arts have been degenerating ever since the Italian artist, Piero Manzoni, canned his own feces in 1961. That's something that had never been done before – it was new – and although I can appreciate Manzoni's statement, especially with regard to commodity fetishism, in the end, what really is there after that? The arts have reached a crisis point in the constant questing for what's new. Anything that "has never been done before" is deemed to have merit. But this kind of art is often created solely for an elitist echelon, leaving the greater public completely disconnected from the art world.

The irony of the situation is that nothing's new any more – and I fall back on one of my favorite musician's lyrics to support this. Michael Stipe, of the band R.E.M., sang, "Run a carbon-black test on my job, and you will find, it's all been said before," back in 1987 on the band's Document album, and I think it rings true. In my opinion, it's all been said and done better in the past, than things are being done now. The ultimate result of this search for the "shock of the new" is that the standards by which art can be evaluated by have been eliminated, and we've been left with an army of artists who have been trained without rudimentary artistic skills – unable to draw, unable to paint, unable to sculpt.

For me, the Roycrofters-At-Large Association upholds the traditional skills that are under risk of being lost to history, and our greatest goal is to retain these skills while aiming at creating relevant work that isn't mired in past historical styles.

As an artist, what is the best piece of advice that you were ever given? What words of inspiration or advice would you offer those who might aspire to follow in your artistic footsteps?

I think the best advice that I ever received as an artist was to accept any criticism – good or bad. Regardless of a critic's commentary or personal opinion – be it positive or negative – there are so many artists in the world that it is meaningful that anyone takes notice and is speaking about your art at all.

Advice that I would give to aspiring artists is not to worry about what's new and what's now. Tastes are fickle and things change. I would encourage them to focus on whether something is good or not – whether something is solid in its conception and is meaningful to them. And most of all I would encourage them not to bother with the opinions of others; you have to be very single-minded to be and artist, and have a tough skin.

When someone looks at something you have created, what type of reaction or emotion do you hope to see, and why?

When someone looks at something that I've created, I hope that the experience somehow moves them. If they can relate what they see in my work to their life, and glean personal understanding from it, that's special and meaningful. The kind of art I gravitate towards, and strive to create, is the kind that is imbued with the highest hopes and ideals for humanity, and if I touch someone's spirit through my paintings, I couldn't be more satisfied.

Photo by Elliott Anderson

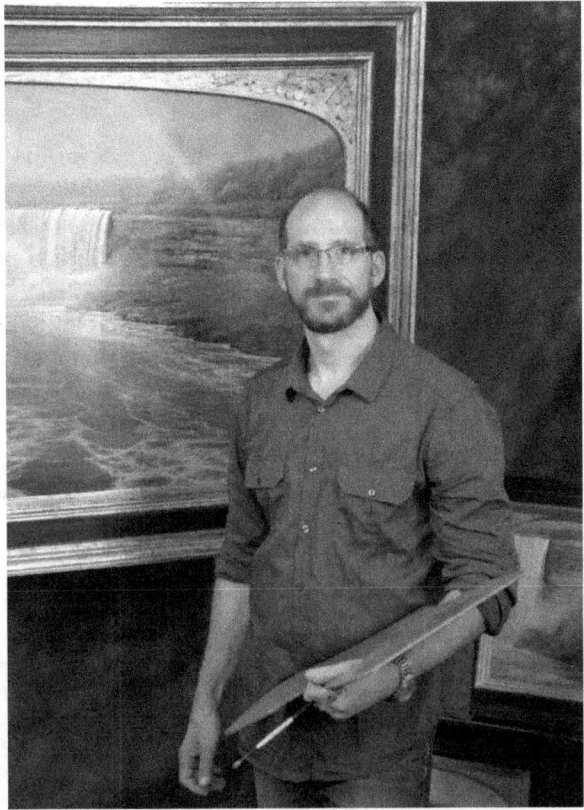

Describe your artistic specialty and what you typically like to create.

I am a Roycroft Master Artisan in painting. My focus is on traditional oil paintings of landscapes, still life and figure.

Describe the space where you typically create, and what is so special about that place?

I work primarily in the studio at my residence in the winter months, and work plein air (outdoors) in the summer. The studio space is designed for a painter with predominant north windows providing a cool and consistent light. It also has wonderful views of the sunrise and sunset that includes a portion of the Sinking Ponds Wildlife Refuge.

I am fortunate to have this space in my house as it allows me to be close to my wife and two children, yet have the ability to be removed enough to focus during painting sessions. My favorite and most informative painting sessions occur outdoors where I draw and paint from life to gather the visual information needed to work on larger studio paintings. It is always refreshing and humbling to paint in the woods.

Where can people see and/or purchase your art?

My recent paintings can be seen on my website at www.thomaskegler.com. I am also very fortunate to have my work represented in numerous galleries throughout the United States, including the John Pence Gallery, San Francisco, California; Trees

Place, Orleans, Massachusetts; Cavalier Galleries, Greenwich, Connecticut; SR Brennen Galleries, Palm Desert, California; Lacuna Galleries, Santa Fe, New Mexico; Edgartwon Art Gallery, Martha's Vineyard, Massachusetts; Beacon Fine Art Gallery, Red Bank, New Jersey; and the Oxford Gallery, Rochester, New York.

Locally, Meibohm Gallery in East Aurora has been featuring my work for many years in both group and solo exhibits.

What is the best piece of advice that you were ever given? What words of inspiration or advice would you offer those who might aspire to follow in your artistic footsteps?

I am a high school art teacher and I instruct numerous landscape and still life workshops in the Northeast. Over the years I have been prompted for words of advice by many of my students.

The best direction I can offer aspiring artists is to find something you are passionate about (both the subject matter and art making medium) and tenaciously immerse yourself. Make art every day and establish a network of like-minded artists. Clarify your vision and set goals. Art making should be a lifestyle, so never stop learning, experimenting and growing. Be humble and share your gifts. Do not pursue creativity and style for their own sake. Pursue truth and beauty — creativity and style will be a bi-product.

As an artist, what has been your most significant achievement, or proudest moment, to date?

Although I love teaching workshops, it is often difficult for individuals to attend due to location and time availability. In an effort to offer the information taught at these classes to a larger audience, I self-produced an instructional documentary DVD focused on landscape painting en plein air several years ago. I am currently filming and editing a second film. This will be an extension of the first film by presenting a studio painting completed for plein air studies. It will walk through the entire process of creating a large-scale studio painting from concept and sketches to framing. The painting is an eight-foot wide depiction of Niagara Falls — my largest painting to date!

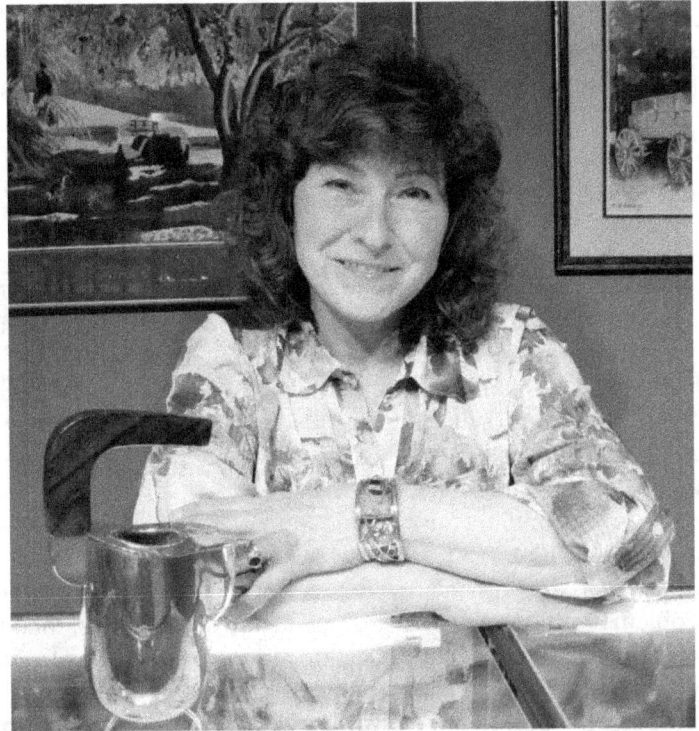

Describe your artistic specialty and what you typically like to create.

Silver and gold, copper and brass, and precious and semi-precious stones are but some of the materials that I craft into wearable art and, generally, functional sculpture. Wearable art, which translates into rings, pendants, bracelets, necklaces and broaches, comprise the majority of my work. I take off on flights of fancy to construct artsy-fartsy containers, impossible rings and sculptural bottle stoppers.

I pick up stones. I pick up bones. I pick up leaves. I look around. I photograph. I daydream. I draw. I erase. I place. I photograph. I contemplate. I rearrange. These are the beginnings of what will become an "object d' art." Or so I'd like to think.

I saw. I hammer. I solder. I file. I sand. I grind. I polish. These are the actions required to craft an object from sheets of metal and lengths of wire. I make stuff and, somehow, some of me gets in there.

Describe when you first truly realized that you had artistic skills, and how you worked to develop those skills.

My mother is a painter so I have her art gene. I would rather do art than math. I would rather do art than make sales calls. I would rather do art than garden. I was always assigned the task of making posters for class functions. I decorated for the prom. Then I went to college and there I was introduced to the most glorious things. Real paint. Real clay. Real photography. Real fiber. Real printmaking. Real metal.

The metal got me. I took metals classes beyond I and II. I made it my craft. I also took metals classes in graduate school and made it my major. I took metal into my home and heart, and I made it my passion.

I received my undergraduate degree in art education and my graduate degree in metals from Ball State University in Muncie, Indiana. Leslie Leupp, who has been the director of the metals program at Penn State since 1988, was my primary instructor.

I was juried into the National Sterling Silver Competition and I had two one-woman shows in galleries in Germany. I have had work in galleries in New York City and Hilton Head Island.

I had a family, and I dropped off the face of the earth.

I taught art in high school — basic art, advanced art, photography and jewelry. Teaching taught me that, at that time, I did not want to teach but to spend my time working with metal.

I unofficially apprenticed with an old jeweler at "Ye Olde Shoppe" in Indianapolis and began to learn what practical bench work was all about. Sizing rings, retipping prongs, repairing bails ... the boring but essential stuff. The challenging stuff.

Then, life took me on another path when I shuffled off to Buffalo. I apprenticed with a production stone setter and was also recruited as a bench jeweler. Production work redefines boring — essential, challenging, repetitive. And don't they say "practice makes perfect?" I'm still practicing.

Fine art metalsmithing and production jewelry work have blended and refined my skills as a metal artisan. I can approach a concept with a clear idea of what it will take to transform that idea into a tangible piece of artwork. The time factor is what I still have problems with. It goes so fast in my head ... just do this, then that, then this. It usually takes me about three times as long to make a piece as I think it will.

What is your attraction to the Roycroft arts community and the Roycrofters-At-Large Association? How has it impacted you as an artist?

Since I have been on both sides of the fence, production jewelry and jewelry as art, the Roycroft arts community appeals strongly to my inclinations to produce high-quality and unique pieces of art by hand. Working in an artistic community striving to promote and uphold the ideals of the original Roycrofters is stimulating. The pieces that they create are inspirational and motivating. The standards of quality that are advocated and expected keep every artisan aware that his or her best efforts are always required. It helps to activate the little voice in one's head asking, "Is it really good enough to be finished? Is this my best effort?"

There is an active appreciation of the Roycroft arts community in East Aurora. The local population has a keen awareness of the Roycroft and its artisans. There is always an influx of visitors who follow the Roycroft Movement, and the ones that don't invariably find it interesting and worthwhile to investigate while they are in the area. It is a point of pride to be a part of the Roycroft Artisans and to be able to share information with other people attracted to learning about not only Roycroft, but my individual craft as well. It is a major point of pride to have earned the designation of Roycroft Master Artisan.

Please share something else related to your craft which was not on this list of questions.

I have collected enough stones, both cabochons and faceted, to last a very long time. I have bone. I have pieces of glass. I have scrap copper tubing. I have beads. I have shells. I have small plastic action figures. I just have all kinds of stuff. My goal is to get to a point in my career, as it were, to be able to come into my studio and say "I think I will just make earrings today." Or, "I think I will begin to finish the three-part series of containers in copper with the bone today." Or, "I think I want to raise another silver bowl. Maybe one with a lid."

My sketchbooks are bursting with ideas. I would like to turn some of them into reality. The need to express ideas and emotions via art runs through me and the vehicle I use to convey these ideas and emotions is metal.

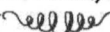
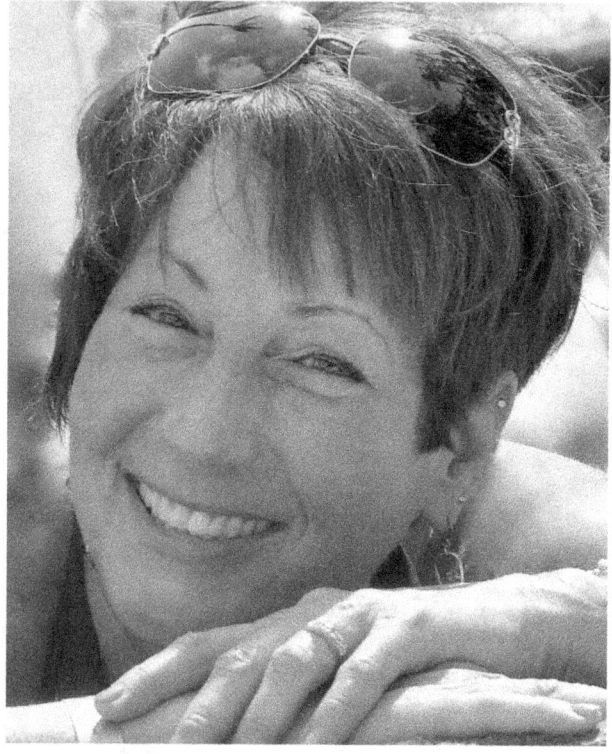

Describe your artistic specialty and what you typically like to create.

Just as a painter adds colors to a canvas, I add layers of molten glass over a stainless steel mandrel, resulting in my miniature masterpiece ... a bead.

Describe when you first truly realized that you had artistic skills, and how you worked to develop those skills.

I have always had a love for art and creating. As a kid I always had a sketchbook with me. I drew everything from the neighbor's barn to faces of friends. When it comes to crafting and do-it-yourself projects, they are my favorite pastimes. Watching TV is an activity I rarely do as there are just so many other things to fill my time with. My day usually involves making or building something. People often say "I'm so lucky to have such a talent," and I laugh because they have no idea. I jokingly say back, "It's more like a curse." Creating is life encompassing. I'm not one to be bored, there are just way too many things to do that involve creating something of some sort.

As a young girl I remember that my grandmother couldn't wait to see my sketchbook. She loved to see what was newly added to the pages. I remember her encouragement to follow my passion for art and embrace it in my adult years. She was college educated, which was uncommon for women in her time period. She wanted to see me continue my education at an art institute after high school. However, my father felt artists were a dime a dozen and that I need to pursue being a secretary or a nurse — something a woman could make a living at, or so he believed.

After high school I worked my way up the business ladder and managed the office for a national general contracting firm for over 10 years. In my late twenties I decided to take a different career path and went back to school to become a Registered Nurse. I worked in nursing for a few years but never felt that is where I belonged. I married in my young thirties, started a family and began my home-based business. My business has evolved many times throughout the past 20 years to become what it is today.

What really made me begin my glass bead-making career occurred about 15 years ago when I saw handmade glass beads for the first time on a friend's bracelet. My eyes lit up and the wheels started to turn. I have been a collector of glass art, mostly paperweights. I've read books about great glass artists of the world. I also have a few of their pieces in my collection as well. Seeing a handmade glass bead was like looking at a paperweight on a much smaller scale. I was so taken by the beauty of this bead; it was art that could be worn and continually admired. Because it was made of glass it would never fade in color or easily be worn out. In a thousand years from now it would almost look the same.

My intrigue quickly turned to fascination. I bought a few books about this particular glass art, which is called "lampworking." Hundreds of years ago, before modern torches were invented, the torch was called a lamp, hence the name lampworking and not torch working. From there it wasn't long before I bought my first torch, some glass and a few simple tools and I was off to melting glass.

My first attempts were some really ugly globs, not even close to being round, and the colors burned to a hideous shade of brown. They weren't pretty but I kept working. If other people could do it, so could I. Practice makes perfect. I kept at it and of course saw improvement, but my early work was very primitive to say the least. Other people thought it was great, but I knew where I wanted my level of work to be and the perfection I was striving for.

I kept researching the internet and other information sources trying to teach myself. There were no local studios or workshops where you could go to for help at the time, so many of the techniques that I have now mastered I have learned completely by accident or trial and error. Sometimes a lot more error than success, but that's OK. In my case, being self-taught is what has driven me to were I am today, and I am still continuing to learn and there is so much more out there to do. There are so many new techniques just waiting for me to discover, and there are so many places to draw inspiration from.

What is your attraction to the Roycroft arts community and the Roycrofters-At-Large Association? How has it impacted you as an artist?

When I first started my bead-making endeavor, my best encouragement was that people actually wanted to buy my beads! They were so well received. Friends and family were actually waiting to see what I made next. It was such a great incentive to keep pushing myself. And to this day I am still pushing myself to continually grow as a glass artist. This is what being a Roycroft Artisan is all about. We are a collective group of artisans working together, encouraging each other, complementing each other, and when it's appropriate, offering constructive criticism.

The personal recognition of obtaining master status in this art community is of the highest level and something I am very proud to have accomplished. I am so fortunate to have been able to work from home within my own glass studio and raise my two daughters. My girls have grown up with this business and my customers have watched them grow up, too. They have always been with me at craft shows since they were small, and now as young women they continue to come with me. I'm so blessed to have a job that I truly love and I can work with my family.

When someone looks at something you have created, what type of reaction or emotion do you hope to see, and why?

I love listening to a customer pick up one of my beads and tell me what they see in it. Sometimes they see what I intentionally made, and sometimes they see something completely different which opens my eyes to a whole new light. So many customers buy one of my pieces because they see something within the glass that triggers a fond memory they have. They share these stories with me and I love hearing them. It brings great pride to know people will love my beads for many years to come.

With that said, beads have always been of great importance to our history. Beads have been found in nearly every aspect of ancient human civilization. They were worn by pharaohs, used as currency and traded on merchant ships. There is an old story (fact or fiction) that Manhattan was purchased for beads from the Dutch. The bead-makers in Holland were themselves Venetians, like their contemporary counterparts in Venice. Bead making has a great historical importance, and I have such an appreciation for the craft. So many people are drawn to beads for so many reasons, whether it's for the historical significance or just the intricate beauty.

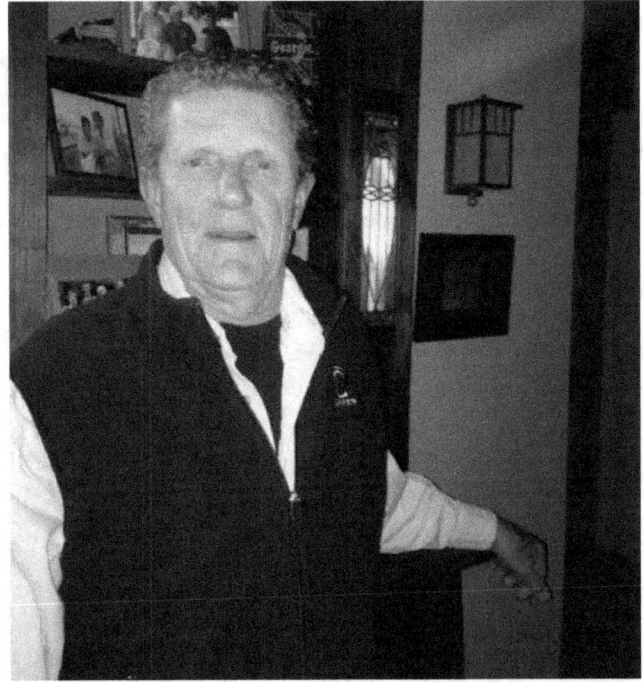

Describe your artistic specialty and what you typically like to create.

I started working with wood as a preteen in my father's basement workshop. I enjoyed creating projects for school which required design and implementation using a combination of hand and power tools. I also enjoyed building models out of both wood and plastic.

When my wife Karen and I bought our first home in East Aurora in 1969, I got involved in remodeling projects in which I had no experience — including specialty furniture pieces for this house as well as designing and building a new kitchen, including cabinets. My time spent working with wood on these projects was very satisfying.

I left a 25-year career with the YMCA to become a cabinet maker. I was mentored by a longtime friend, Tom Harris. Tom and I discovered that we worked well together. We became partners and opened the Schoolhouse Gallery and Cabinet Shop in 1987. Our 27-year partnership continued until Tom retired in 2013.

I discovered that I really liked creating dining tables because of their ability to bring families together. In addition to making tables for customers, I also enjoy creating and making beds. Over the years, in addition to creating tables and beds for customers, I have designed eight dining room tables and 16 beds in a variety of styles for our extended family. I really enjoy knowing that these tables and beds will be in use, even after my chair is empty.

Describe the space where you typically create, and what is so special about that place?

When I first left my career with the YMCA, my intention was to build a shop in our barn on Liberia Road in Marilla, New York. However, friends from the YMCA started asking me to create pieces for their homes. As a result I started to lean on my friend Tom Harris for advice, for use of his tools and for assistance with some of my commissions. We quickly learned that we worked well together.

Tom had his shop in a 1850's one-room schoolhouse at 1054 Olean Road, East Aurora. We added a pole barn that we could use as a shop and the schoolhouse became a gallery for our works and those of other artisans. We formed a partnership and created the Schoolhouse Gallery and Cabinet Shop. Tom and I were partners for 27 years and completed hundreds of pieces that are in homes, schools and churches all over the United States.

Our shop and gallery are special to me for a number of reasons. I have always enjoyed working in a location that has significant history. I also have enjoyed adding to the history of the location. The shop is in a rural setting just outside the Village of East Aurora and has provided us with a wonderful work space in which we were able to create many beautiful pieces.

Tom Harris retired and our official New York State business ended in 2013. I still own the shop and artisan gallery and share ownership of the property with my Roycroft Master Artisan partner, Thomas Pafk. I look forward to continuing to create pieces for family and friends.

What is your attraction to the Roycroft arts community and the Roycrofters-At-Large Association? How has it impacted you as an artist?

I have been interested in the Roycroft arts community and the association since becoming a Roycroft Artisan in 1989. I have been committed to carrying on the history and philosophy of Elbert Hubbard and the original Roycrofters throughout my career. As a Roycroft Master Artisan I have always tried to incorporate the philosophy of "Head, Heart and Hand" in my work and in my life.

Throughout my journey as an artisan I have reflected Roycroft in the quality of my work, in my involvement in the Roycrofters-At-Large Association, and in community activities that have helped interpret and preserve Roycroft. I am a lifetime member of the organization and was president for four years during the renovation of the Roycroft Inn. I developed an East Aurora night school class called Little Journeys that brought the "old" and the "new" Roycroft together.

With fellow Roycroft Master Artisan Tom Harris we developed a hands-on shop experience for fourth and fifth grade students from Iroquois and East Aurora schools. This program involved learning about the history of Roycroft as well as creating and constructing a project. I did extensive research on the original Roycroft Cabinet Shop and Herb Buffum, who was the superintendent of the Cabinet Shop in the early 1900s. I have presented the history of the Cabinet Shop in first person as Herb Buffum to historical societies, Roycroft Elderhostel/Roads Scholars, school groups and other groups in Western New York.

Also, I am currently a docent at Frank Lloyd Wright's Graycliff. As a docent I incorporate Roycroft history as it relates to Graycliff and the Darwin Martin family. As you can see, Roycroft has not only affected my work but it has worked itself in to my life.

As an artist, what has been your most significant achievement, or proudest moment, to date?

During a career span of over 27 years, I have created many pieces and jobs of which I am extremely proud and feel were significant achievements.

Schoolhouse Gallery was commissioned in the design, creation and installation of four Arts and Crafts-style libraries. The first library was for East Aurora High School. The job included library tables, dictionary and atlas stands, and display cases for rare books and was created from quarter-sawn white oak.

The second library was for Iroquois High School. This project included round library tables, a desk for the librarian, dictionary stands and a circulation desk. This project was created from black cherry and tiger maple.

The third and largest library project, which lasted for two years, was for City Honors School in Buffalo, New York. This project included library tables, dictionary and atlas stands, computer desks/work stations and a large circulation desk. In addition to the library, the project involved a front office desk and file cabinet surrounds. The entire project was created from quarter-sawn white oak.

The fourth library was created for Frederick Law Olmsted School in Buffalo, New York. This project included library tables, dictionary and atlas stands, and was created out of quarter-sawn white oak.

All pieces for all libraries have the Roycroft Renaissance mark engraved in prominent locations. Contrary to the naysayers, the teenage students have shown great respect, care and pride for this furniture.

I am not only proud of the pieces that were created for these schools, but I also feel fondly about the City Honors and Frederick Law Olmsted projects as they were the last two projects completed by the Schoolhouse Gallery.

Please share something else related to your craft which was not on this list of questions.

When I left my 25-year career with the YMCA in my early forties many people asked, "Why the change?" and "How did you have the nerve to do this?" To answer their questions, I explained that in the beginning I chose the YMCA to work with people and sadly, towards the end of my career, I felt I was a "paper pusher." I had always enjoyed working with my hands and had thoughts about starting my own business as a cabinet maker. Thanks to my fellow Master Artisan Tom Harris, I decided to follow my dream.

My wife Karen and I decided to try this for a year and if it didn't work I would find something else. Thankfully it worked for 27 years as a career and I am still enjoying being a Roycroft Master Artisan, working in my shop and creating pieces for family. When we built our retirement home in Colorado in 1997 I created each piece of Arts and Crafts-style furniture in my shop in East Aurora and over the years transported it out to Colorado. Every day I can enjoy my achievements in every room of our house.

My woodworking career has been a mix of labor and leisure as reflected in this quote: "The master in the art of living makes little distinction between his work and his play, his labor and his leisure, his mind and his body, his information and his recreation, his love and his religion. He hardly knows which is which. He simply pursues his vision of excellence at whatever he does, leaving others to decide whether he is working or playing. To him, he's always doing both." Author unknown.

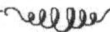

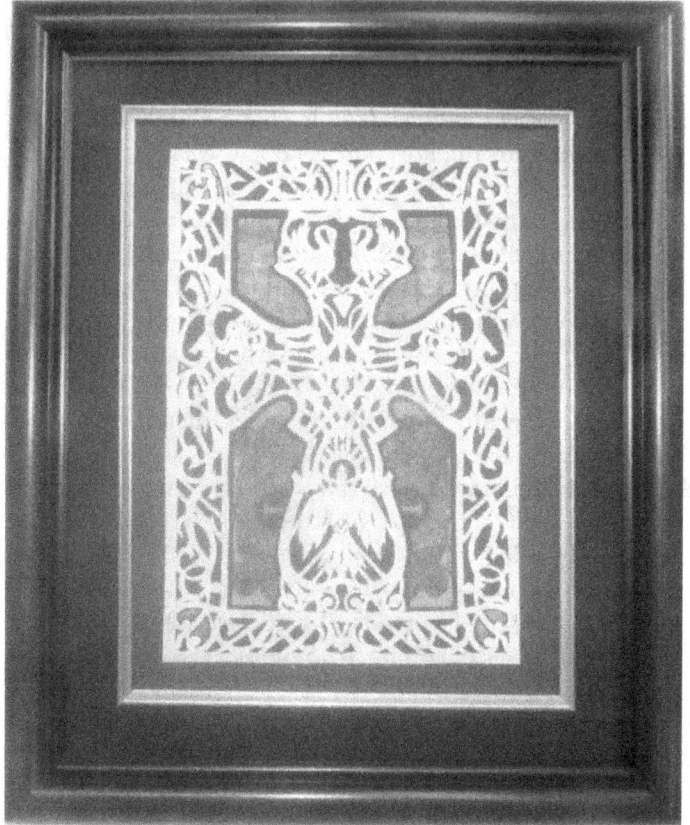

Describe your artistic specialty and what you typically like to create.

For the last 20-plus years I have researched, designed and exhibited a body of work composed entirely of paper. Initially I worked exclusively in classical paper cutting techniques. These pieces were effective in presenting hard-edged, high-contrast imagery suitable for illustration and commemorative works.

Then these pieces fell under the category of Scherenschnitte, a European art form brought to this country in the mid 1700s. In response, to convey a more complex level of meaning and expression, I began to search for a way to incorporate varying paper techniques in a single work. This, coupled with my consuming interest in the science of paper making and the historical use of paper, led me to explore many paths of paper manipulation and decoration. These paths have come together in many surprising and unique compositions.

A paper cutting can be simply hand-colored, or textures can be drawn into the piece. Often I add old currency, Valentines and other vintage papers throughout the piece. Other techniques used are printmaking, embossing, collage and paper casting.

My design sources are just as varied. Storytelling is an essential component. The objective or philosophy of my work is to preserve ideas that have been for the most part forgotten but are worthwhile. I like to create a thread from generation to generation. That is why I have included Biblical passages, hymns, fables and Roycroft mottos as subject matter. Other pieces capture the mood or spirit of the songs and poems from childhood. In many cases the words are cut into the piece itself.

I create special designs for retirements, marriages, anniversaries, births, memorials and really unique items for special occasions.

Who/what are your inspirations, and why?

My family and my faith in Christ are my main sources of inspiration. My dad, who is very well read, instilled a love of classic literature which many of my designs are based on. My mom indulged me by allowing me free range to create at the kitchen table while she worked and provided me with an array of art materials. My grandpa was the first to frame my artwork and hang it in his office.

Describe the space where you typically create, and what is so special about that place?

When we added to our home we had one room done specifically as my studio space with large windows for lots of light and lots of room to spread out the papers I use in my work.

What is your attraction to the Roycroft arts community and the Roycrofters-At-Large Association? How has it impacted you as an artist?

I became a Roycroft Artisan in 1986. At that time the Roycroft Artisans were like an extended family — noncompetitive, open and very nurturing to a new artist.

Where can people see and/or purchase your art?

People can purchase my work at shows, the Copper Shop and by visiting my studio.

When someone looks at something you have created, what type of reaction or emotion do you hope to see, and why?

The pieces are designed with levels of symbolism not only in the details, but in the overall construction of the composition. I hope that the piece will inspire reflection and contemplation and that the viewer will make new discoveries in the piece over time.

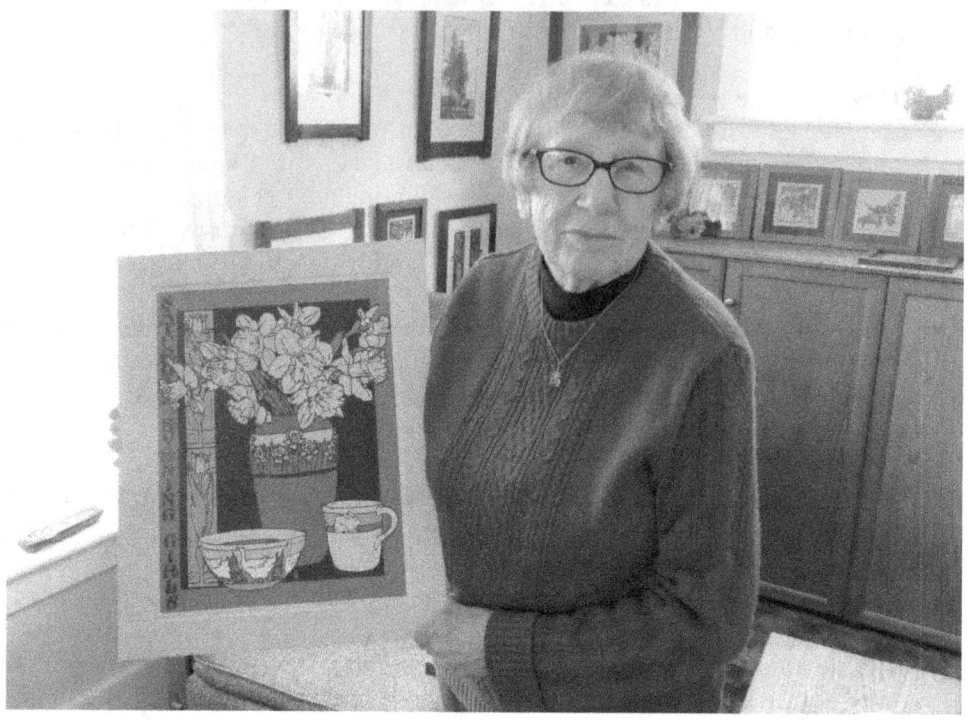

Describe your artistic specialty and what you typically like to create.

I am a Roycroft Renaissance Master Artisan, Emeritus, and I am too old to do shows anymore. I have painted with oils, acrylics, watercolors and pastels, and won numerous awards throughout Western New York.

I am a printmaker specializing in screen printing. I have exhibited and taught classes here in Hamburg, as well as at the Chautauqua Institution, the Copper Shop and the Power House, and I have given presentations at the Darwin Martin House Gardener's Cottage and for art groups all over Western New York.

I have a print in the permanent collection of the Burchfield-Penny Art Center as well as many private and public collections. I have also developed my own techniques to print on both paper and fabric; I design and print small editions of 20 to 50. These are often garden and field flowers in collectible Arts and Crafts pottery with related borders that suggest friezes of the period. I only use the best materials and mat my prints archaically. Those who bought my prints years ago tell me that they look as they did when new.

Describe when you first truly realized that you had artistic skills, and how you worked to develop those skills.

I have always been an artist. Years ago when I moved to Western New York, I had an immediate impression of the strong character of the buildings and landscape in this area. I started using screen printing to express what I saw and felt. I found that breaking down images into areas of flat color strengthened my work. That led me to experiment — printing on different surfaces and using a variety of stencil making techniques. I printed everything: landscapes, historical architecture, portraits, nature studies and quilt patterns.

Because of my strong interest in the period, I have designed my recent work to have an Arts and Crafts look. I find screen printing a very personal way to create art. The craft, the hands-on work, is every bit as important and satisfying as the aesthetic vision. There is always something new to discover whenever I am creating my own work or teaching.

Who/what are your inspirations, and why?

Arthur Wesley Dow inspired me as well as many other more well-known artists. I also go to my garden for inspiration — many of my prints are of flowers in my garden.

Describe the space where you typically create, and what is so special about the place?

I have a basement studio where I do printing, matting and framing. I will be giving this up when I move to a smaller, more manageable space.

Please share something else related to your craft which was not on this list of questions.

I get much joy in seeing people's reactions to my work.

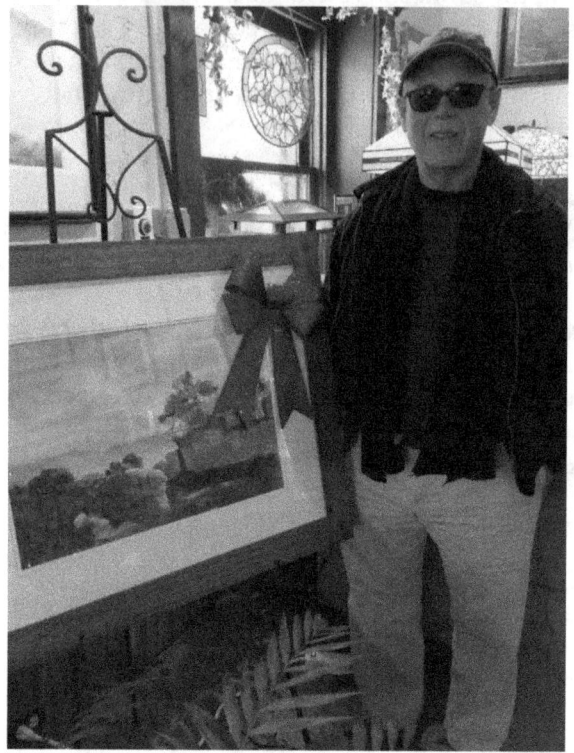

Describe your artistic specialty and what you typically like to create.

My Roycroft Master Artisan specialty is watercolor paintings and ink drawings. I have been working in these media for over 40 years and was accepted as a Roycroft Artisan in 2001.

My watercolors are done in several styles, depending on the subject matter, but my landscapes have always tended to be made in the Arts and Crafts style, even before I knew that there was such a style.

My landscapes are influenced by the painters and printmakers of ancient China and Japan and the group of artists sometimes known as the California Tonalists of the early 1900s. My favorite landscape subjects include the Central Coast area of California, Big Sur and the coast of Maine. Using muted tones, earthy colors and delicately balanced minimalist compositions, I try to convey a quiet sense of peace with an air of mystery. I try to capture the atmosphere of a place.

Who/what are your inspirations, and why?

Two artists have been my primary inspiration: Winslow Homer and Ray Ellis. Although Homer is better known for his oils, I have always admired his watercolors. Seeing his watercolors was one of the earliest awakenings of the desire to make watercolors myself.

I saw Ray Ellis's watercolors in the 1970s in two coffee table books in which he had illustrated two East Coast sailing trips that he and Walter Cronkite had sailed together, with Cronkite writing a journal of the trips. Both artists were early and ongoing influences.

Describe the space where you typically create, and what is so special about that place?

I have had several studios over the years and find that I can enjoy working in almost any studio that is quiet, has a minimum of 100 square feet of floor space and is not located in a cold basement. Painting outside on location has a few negatives, but looking back on it I realize that some of my favorite pieces were created en plein air.

What is your attraction to the Roycroft arts community and the Roycrofters-At-Large Association? How has it impacted you as an artist?

I discovered the organization after many years of painting on my own in the style of Arts and Crafts, and was happy to find a group of like-minded artisans.

Where can people see and/or purchase your art?

Four galleries presently show my works: The Artisan Gallery in the old Schoolhouse Gallery in East Aurora, New York; The Copper Shop Gallery on the Roycroft Campus, East Aurora, New York; The Watercolor Gallery in Laguna Beach, California; and Camden Falls Gallery in Camden, Maine. My works are also available through my website, www.BobMauer.com.

As an artist, what is the best piece of advice that you were ever given? What words of inspiration or advice would you offer those who might aspire to follow in your artistic footsteps?

The best advice I have is to continually work at improving your craft, and enjoy the work.

As an artist, what has been your most significant achievement, or proudest moment, to date?

The achievements that have given me the most satisfaction were: 1. Being accepted as a Roycroft Artisan some 15 years ago, and 2. Being accepted as a Roycroft Master Artisan in my first year of eligibility.

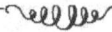

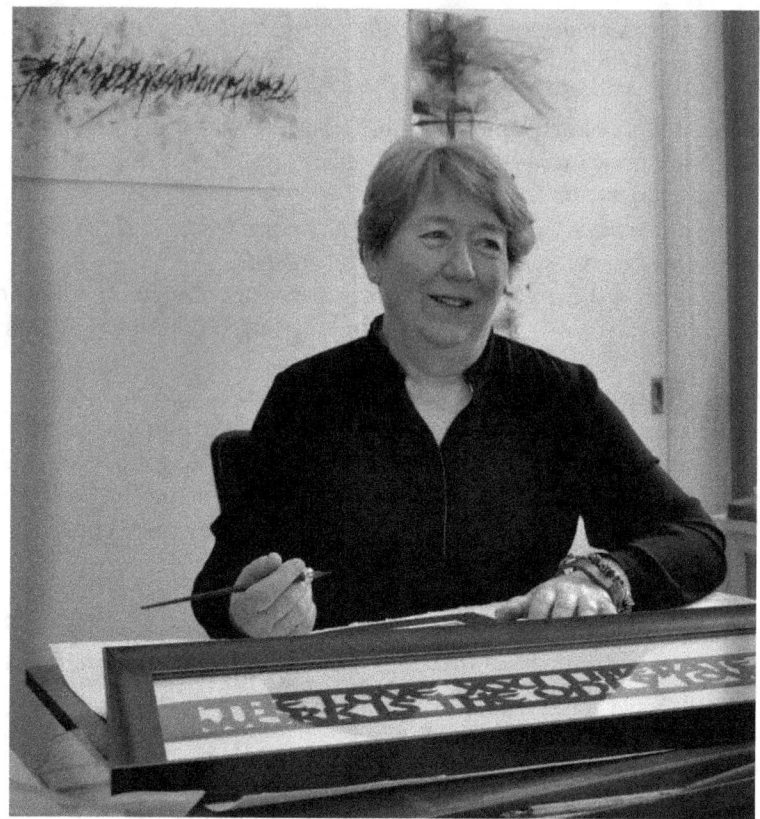

Describe your artistic specialty and what you typically like to create.

My medium is calligraphy. Defined as the "art of beautiful writing," it has been part of my life for more than 35 years. Even before I knew what calligraphy truly was, I was experimenting with it in my everyday life. As a teen and young working woman, my personal handwriting frequently underwent changes. I would decide to make a "t" in a certain way, or tilt my letters backwards, or make them as tiny as possible. I was constantly experimenting with my writing and trying to make a visual statement with it.

I love quotations and words and letters of all shapes and sizes. I generally do what are referred to as "broadsides" — poems or quotations that are designed to be framed and enjoyed as art. But I also love the prospect of hand lettering and creating one-of-a-kind books and cards. These smaller pieces invite a more intimate interaction with the reader and are actually more terrifying to produce. If someone is going to hold that piece in their hands, they can see where the pen might have skipped or the ink blobbed; they might notice that your slant was off in some places and they might even recognize that you've changed the way you make your "e" from one line to the next. But there's something much richer in the experience of having them touch the paper, turn the pages and read words that have been put there by another hand — not a machine.

Describe when you first truly realized that you had artistic skills, and how you worked to develop those skills.

I'm not sure if, at first, I thought I had any artistic skills. I had taken a few art courses in high school and college, but was much more involved with music and writing. I always liked art and design and thought I had a pretty good eye for a well-executed piece, but I don't remember ever getting any sort of encouragement about art projects I had completed.

However, I remember vividly when I first discovered calligraphy and knew that I wanted to do it — no matter what. I was covering an art opening as a freelance writer and walked into an exhibition of calligraphy. I was enthralled. With two degrees in English, I had saved many wonderful quotations and had several notebooks full of them. I knew immediately that calligraphy would let me do something visual with all those words I loved. I started my first class with the artist whose work I had been assigned to cover. As I moved to new jobs I always seemed to find new calligraphy instructors and new things to study.

Like any skill, it takes time to become proficient. Your fingers need to learn the feel of the pen and your eye needs to recognize the shapes of letters and the spaces between letters that make up words. I still practice. I still take classes, still enjoy finding new tools. I still love the act of putting letters on paper with either ink or pencil.

The Roycrofters referred to craft as head, hand and heart all working together. That is so true. Beginning calligraphy students will often remark during even their first class that their letters don't look right. Their eyes quickly distinguish a difference, but their hand may not be cooperating! That's where practice comes in. When you finally "get it," the whole process should look simple. It should look like the letters just flow out of your fingers without effort.

What is your attraction to the Roycroft arts community and the Roycrofters-At-Large Association? How has it impacted you as an artist?

Becoming a Roycroft Artisan was a defining moment in my life and has made me infinitely better at my art. I am much more self-critical and frequently rework pieces that I once would have said were "good enough." Being part of a group whose members all produce incredible pieces makes you conscious of maintaining your own level of expertise. You stop and think if it's worthy of receiving the Roycroft mark.

What continually amazes me when the Roycroft Master Artisans convene to jury new prospects is the innate ability everyone seems to have to recognize truly excellent workmanship — no matter what the medium. The woodworkers can value the effort that a needleworker has put into a quilt; the coppersmiths appreciate the detail and precision in a carved woodblock print; jewelers will run their hands over the perfectly sanded surface of a wooden table. They may not know how to create these works themselves, but they inherently understand the quality of the workmanship and the skill of the maker.

I like being part of a long tradition that appreciates the beauty of things made by hand.

Where can people see and/or purchase your art?

I primarily sell through the Copper Shop Gallery on the Roycroft Campus. I do only one or two shows a year — all local. I have a website but do not sell items from it at this time. I am not very prolific and almost everything I sell is an original piece of art. I only rarely do prints of my work.

When someone looks at something you have created, what type of reaction or emotion do you hope to see, and why?

First of all, I know that calligraphy is not for everyone! You have to love words and want to have them in your home as part of your life ... the text really has to "speak" to you. My repeat customers generally share stories about who they have given cards to, what authors they like and often provide me with wonderful new quotations that I add to my notebooks. There is a kindred spirit among those of us who have a love of words.

I enjoy having people watch me letter because it is a skill that is becoming lost. Dipping a pen into a bottle of ink and making marks on a piece of paper is not part of our everyday life any more. People often ask very specific and insightful questions about writing with pen and ink.

However, when offered a chance to try it, most adults are too timid and too afraid of making a mistake to pick up the pen. Children, on the other hand, love it. One of the best comments I have ever received was an enthusiastic "that is so cool" from a 12-year-old boy who tried writing with a goose feather quill dipped into ink made from black walnuts. As keyboarding takes over and the act of writing in cursive even with a ballpoint pen is being lost, I hope that he will long remember the feel of writing with those traditional tools.

Photo by Theresa Day

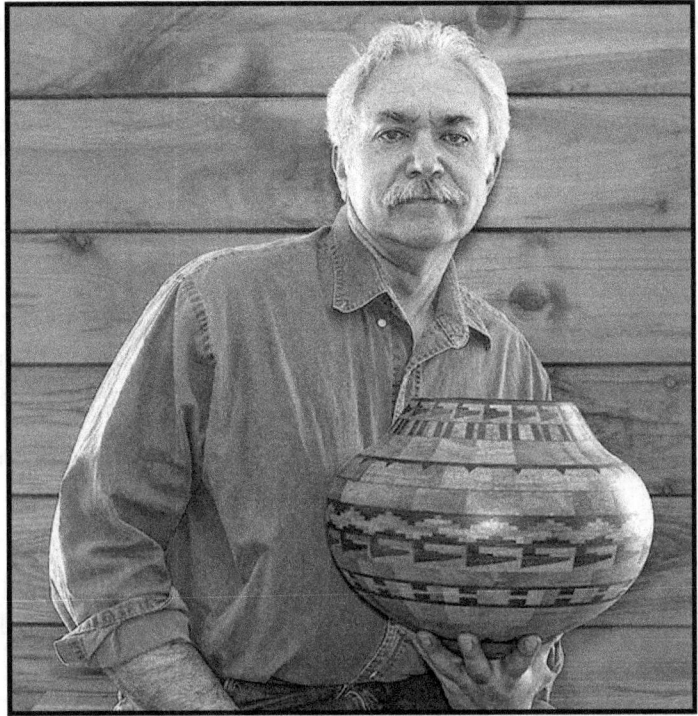

Describe your artistic specialty and what you typically like to create.

My specialty for the last six years has been segmented wood turning. Wood turning is mounting a piece of wood (can be various materials) on a lathe which spins the work piece while the operator shapes it with different tools such as gouges, scrapers and skew chisels.

The segmented part is that I glue various pieces of naturally colored woods to make patterns and designs. I use Native American designs and symbols from the Southwest's Four Corners region of the United States. I research them through books and the internet then re-create them using glued pieces of wood. In essence, I make wooden Indian pottery — nonfunctional art but something different as people are used to pottery from clay. Each piece has between 650 and 1,200 pieces of wood in them.

I also have been making segmented Christmas ornaments since the early nineties. They are comprised of a globe with a finial top and an icicle shape at the bottom. The globes are approximately 2.25 inches in diameter and the icicle is around 5 to 5.5 inches long. The globes are hollow and the whole thing weighs in at around 1.75 ounces. I do have quite a few collectors of these ornaments so every year there are at least two to four new color combinations for them to pick from. Every ornament, like the bowls and pots, is signed and dated.

One specific challenge is putting pieces of colored wood together that complement each other. Unfortunately, sometimes it is trial and error. You can put two boards next to each other and get an idea of what they will look like together, but when they are turned, sanded and finished they may look somewhat different so you have to learn which to use, and when. It sometimes takes longer to pick out the wood than it does to draw up the plans.

Describe when you first truly realized that you had artistic skills, and how you worked to develop those skills.

All my life it seems I have done something on the artistic side. It was either drawing, painting or building something. Pen and ink was my preferred media along with pencil sketching. I tried my hand at oil and watercolor painting but did not have any knack for them.

When I entered junior high I was introduced to a formal art class and an actual shop class for the first time. Although I enjoyed drawing and working with wood I was totally not interested in either class. I found it hard to be creative on cue and just to finish assignments as we were very limited on what we could do in shop class. I passed both but hated them. I did, however, become interested in mechanical drafting and architectural drawing. These stayed with me and are what I use extensively in my pottery making now.

As far as my woodworking, I have dealt with the question of art and artistic ability for the past few years. The more serious I got about what I do, the more the question pops up. I see my work as making artistic objects but do not know how artistic the process is. It starts with the research then the drawing of the blueprint. After that comes lumber selection, which seems to be the most artistic part. Then it goes to the mechanical part of cutting, sanding, gluing, and finally turning and finishing.

I have studied and use phi and the golden ratio to make sure the overall shapes are pleasing to the eye. Native Americans had that ability naturally, it seems.

The other reason I may have difficulty with the arts question is my thinking is more linear and not as free-flowing as I think it should be. Also, many of the designs I am interpreting are geometric in shape and I am making them out of wood rather than painting them.

Describe the space where you typically create, and what is so special about that place?

I work in my shop which is in the basement of my home, and I use about 1,400 square feet of it. When my wife and I built the house I had the basement walls poured a foot higher than normally done to accommodate a shop with a little better head clearance.

The shop is broken up into five areas, the largest one being for the stationary power tools such as table saw, planer, drum sander and lathe. This area is further broken into sub areas for cutting, sanding, assembly and turning. Each space has its own work bench with sets of tools for the job at that station, which saves walking from one to the other to get commonly used tools.

The next space is a cubicle-type arrangement that contains my drawing board and desk. Then there is the insulated dust collection room that I put up so the dust collector was not so loud. Every stationary machine in the shop is connected to the dust collector.

The fourth area is for lumber and veneer storage and is shared with a finishing booth for the spraying of finishes. The fifth and final area contains a cutting table and veneer press. The cutting table is for cutting veneers and cardboard for templates or anything else that can be cut with a utility knife, and the vacuum press is for veneered pieces.

When someone looks at something you have created, what type of reaction or emotion do you hope to see, and why?

To be honest, the first and best response to something I have created would be to reach for their wallets. I will, however, settle for stunned amazement and jaw-dropping awe.

All that aside I really want them to see and appreciate what I have actually done. Most people pick up that I am re-creating Indian pottery out of wood and think it is different and unique. Also, I want them to notice the tightness of joints and the quality of the finishing.

It also surprises them that the colors of the wood are natural. Then come the questions of how they are done, so I have several examples of work in various stages of completion to help them understand a small part of the process.

I had a lady come into my booth in Chicago and ask me where I got my clay from. I did not catch on for a few seconds that she did not realize the pots were wood, then informed her of what they were really made of ... and the look on her face was priceless! To have a design or pattern that is good enough that people think it is painted is a compliment to me, just as I have had people think my Christmas ornaments are made from glass.

As an artist, what has been your most significant achievement, or proudest moment, to date?

There is no one achievement or single proudest moment. I look at any special moment as a step up and make sure to do my best to keep them coming. I appreciate winning best in show at the Allentown Art Festival in Buffalo and completing a new pot that is even better in front of me than it looked on paper. My wife told me years ago that a pot that I love and am proud of should be the norm, not the exception. No pressure there!

Many things come into play when making these designs, such as wood selection, grain orientation and sanding. I still find it thrilling to successively complete a design that I have drawn, and by the same token feel that being accepted as a Master Artisan in the Roycroft guild is a milestone of my work.

Another exciting time is working with the Martin House Restoration Corporation on several ongoing projects. To be able to do that and be considered to have the quality they require is a big step for me. I continue to work for the next step up.

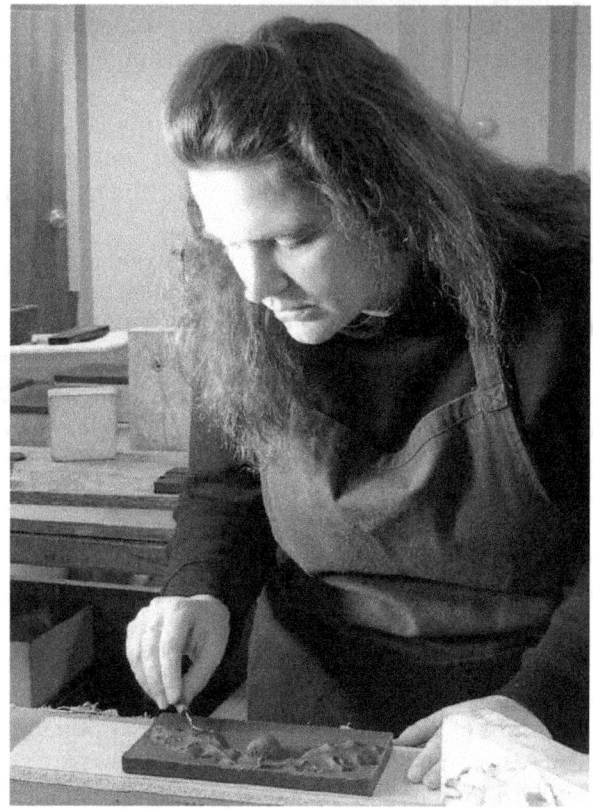

Describe your artistic specialty and what you typically like to create.

My Roycroft Master Artisan award is in clay and my primary concentration is in "decorative tile." I design and create hundreds of decorative tiles yearly which can be used in many applications. Many folks will use my tiles as accents or focal points in a home installation such as a fireplace surround or a kitchen backsplash.

Another extremely popular way my tiles are used is as decorative art wall hangings. As "Mission Guild Studio," my partner James and I will collaborate on our work frequently; James is a Roycroft Master Artisan in wood and designs and creates all of the unique frames for our tiles. My tiles are also available to be purchased individually (loose) and make wonderful collectibles/keepsakes.

I primarily work in a red clay body but that's not to say I will not create some of my tiles in white clay. The color of the clay will influence the color and texture of a glaze desired so I will switch from red to white clay depending on the outcome I wish to achieve.

The style of my work falls within the realm of the Arts and Crafts era but also moves beyond. I design simplified forms that make a bold statement. Many of my tile designs will have a graphic designer's approach; many have the look of an Asian block print using the dark silhouette of imagery against a colored background. My motifs are very straightforward so to speak — simplified, stylized shapes and not a lot of clutter.

Trees and forest themes are a big part of my portfolio as well as dragonflies, owls, flowers and mottos. From time to time we will also cast natural botanicals to be worked into my designs, such as flowers, leaves, acorns, pinecones, etc. These castings are extremely challenging as the botanicals are quite delicate and careful handling is key to handcrafting. When everything falls into place these castings create striking, high relief, breathtaking displays.

Describe when you first truly realized that you had artistic skills, and how you worked to develop those skills.

If I really think back, I cannot tell you when I didn't have art in my life. I grew up in a very artistic family as both of my parents were creative; my mother was also a very talented artist in both drawing and painting. My parents kept my sister, brother and I busy creating, imagining, adventuring. Life was very different then with no Internet, no cellphones ... heck, no phones without a long, curly chord.

We made most all of our Christmas gifts for family members as well as a great deal of our holiday decorations. Throughout my childhood and adolescent years I just knew I wanted to be an artist. After high school I went on to study art in college, earning a bachelor's degree in art history from the State University of New York at Oneonta with a concentration in sculpture and design, and an honorable Phi Theta Kappa associate's degree from Cazenovia College in Cazenovia, New York, with a concentration in commercial art and illustration.

During my college years art continued to flow through my veins and no matter what I did in school, at work or in my personal life, it just poured out. I recall it was right after college graduation that I purchased my first ceramic kiln. A very small used kiln, it was a big event in this artist's life. I began then to experiment with clay and glaze on my own time, outside the classroom and institutional setting. From then on life was one big experiment to make a living. Trial and error was a weekly event. It was and is still exciting to create a piece and open the final kiln firing (the glaze firing) to see the big reveal. I always tell our clients that opening a kiln is like Christmas morning ... you never truly know how the gifts will be and it's always a big surprise.

Where can people see and/or purchase your art?

As Mission Guild Studio, my partner James and I sell the majority of our offerings online. We first started our online business many, many moons ago when the dot-com world was being born. I'd say it was around 1998 when I began learning web design and created our first Mission Guild web page within the year.

At that point, buying online via a shopping cart was not really happening yet so everything was viewed online and then sold over the phone. Later we opted to "get out there" a little; working full-time as an artist and working and selling online can bring about a hermit-like feel. James and I are both people persons so getting out was necessary every few months. We started exhibiting in about two to three shows a year in 2003.

Within a couple of years we were exhibiting in about eight shows a year, which we later found out in our line of work was a bit too much — you need time to function, breathe, create and replenish. And when you're creating selections as individuals — not factories — and by hand, studio/home time is extremely important. We've now narrowed show life down to approximately six shows yearly, which is plenty.

I recall one of my most memorable shows was my first. It was at that event a woman purchased one of my first framed forest tile pieces, an amazing piece with rich autumn colors and dark trees. This woman was overwhelmed with our work and said to me, "Are you a Roycrofter?" I was unaware of what she meant; to be honest, at that time we had no idea that there were current Roycrofters even in existence. She wrote a little info on a piece of paper about East Aurora and then I made a note in my sales book to start researching it when I returned home. The rest is history.

If folks are interested in seeing our work in person and/or making a purchase, we have offerings for sale year-round at a few of the historical gallery shops in East Aurora, New York, and on the historic Roycroft Campus. We also have a vast and well established online catalog with online shopping available 24 hours a day, seven days a week. Our website is www.MissionGuild.com. Online you can view and purchase many of our tiles, framed tiles, framed prints, jewelry offerings, furnishings and more. We are always creating new and one-of-a-kind offerings so the website, gallery shops, shows and our life is ever changing.

As an artist, what has been your most significant achievement, or proudest moment, to date?

Most significant achievement to date ... well, that could very well be existence! Life as an artist is not easy. It's not playing with paints and lots of playtime and bright sunny days, especially if you live year-round in upstate New York. Tough weather and winters are par for the course, as well as a lack of sunlight. Being an artist full time and being married to an artist who also creates for a living is no easy task. You basically work on commission — if it sells you live, and if it does not sell ... well, you'd better keep creating because you need to survive.

I think the need to survive is a driving force within both my husband and I, but also the fact that both of us have no shortage of ideas. We are constantly brainstorming — the ideas are ever flowing and we both know we will never create all the ideas we have before we leave this planet. Our business motto from the onset is "Forward Thinking, In The Craftsman Tradition," and that is exactly what we do every day. You need to be on your toes, embracing new worlds, new techniques, new tools and materials. When something does not appear to work for the public, you need to accept that and move on.

Retaining that knowledge you gained from creating that piece, or in some cases pieces, and then start creating anew ... many times we find later that we go back to that knowledge pile and pull out a few key ingredients which blossom into the great idea. If the public does not get excited over a work of art you spent months on, that's not to say that same work would not be embraced in a different town or at a different time. You cannot take things too personally as that will surely seal your fate. It's key to listen to the people when they see your works and watch the people ... watch how they look at it. Body language is key; listen to what they say to you or to their friends next to them. Digest it and then develop it further.

Not every new form is the best and also I have found at the same time one's least favorite can be the first to sell. Stay positive! One of our favorite sayings, especially if times get tough: "Positive brings positive. Negative brings negative." That part is quite simple.

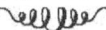
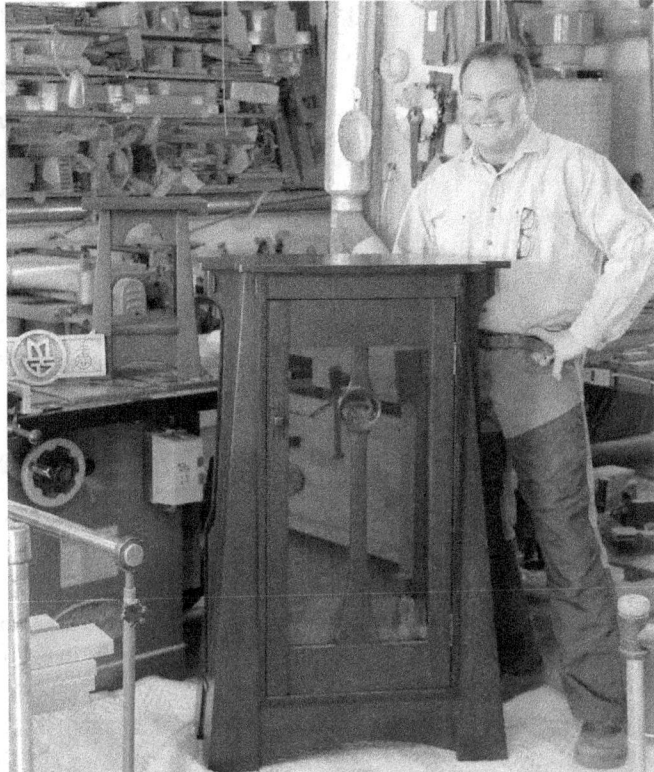

Describe your artistic specialty and what you typically like to create.

Being a Roycroft Master in wood encourages me to create period-style furniture and framing in the Arts and Crafts form and beyond, but I specialize in Arts and Craft period-style work. Quarter-sawn white oak is normally the wood of choice for this work although I can and have worked with many other species. White oak, when quarter-sawn, is very stable and strong and lends itself well to be used for many purposes, from boat ribs to furniture and frames. The first airplanes had frames made from white oak. This species also has a special ingredient within its cells, "tannic acid," that reacts with the fumes of ammonia, changing its color. The early way of coloring oak used this method and gives white oak a specific appearance true to the period. I finish my work in this method exclusively.

My partner Christie and I collaborate in creating unique, one-of-a-kind artworks consisting of joining her handcrafted art tile and my deliberate frame designs to make a combined offering.

Furniture also emerges from our studio as inspiration beckons and time allows. All joinery is true mortise and tenon locked in place with black walnut pegs. My finish is all hand-rubbed and robust. There will be very few or only one of my designs ever produced to ensure high collectibility for the future. If history repeats itself (as it nearly always has), the few or the one will be most sought after, especially if it were signed by the artist.

All work bearing the licensed **RR** mark will give significant value to the quality and collectibility of the work. The Roycroft Renaissance artists represent a unique group who have earned this title by proving their abilities continuously in front of a jury of their peers. This ensures a high level of workmanship and competency, which is the measure of collectibility we seek.

Describe when you first truly realized that you had artistic skills, and how you worked to develop those skills.

Somewhere around 8 to 10 years old, I was featured in a hardcover art book displaying my "string design" I made at camp. I looked funny with my plaid bell bottoms and Dutch Boy haircut, but it's the first recorded moment of art in my life.

My father, Joseph, was owner of a flooring store in Long Island and was said to have installed most of the floors in the county. I was his helper for many of those jobs and learned what hard work meant and the rewards that could come from it.

Who/what are your inspirations, and why?

I am most inspired by those designers who can capture a timeless quality in their work. If when looking upon a piece one cannot date it visually to a certain era, it becomes an enigma and creates intrigue. Charles Rennie Mackintosh designs have this quality.

Describe the space where you typically create, and what is so special about that place?

In the beginning, when we first decided to become "artists" full time, my workshop was knicknamed "tent city" due to the fact we were at that point renting a half garage with a vast network of outdoor tarp buildings connected together. It looked ghastly but served us well in the time where we were uncertain of the viability of our dream.

As soon as we could we moved to an old but beautiful Victorian with a carriage barn for the wood shop and studio space in the main house. Six years later we knew we had again run out of space. We later stumbled upon and purchased an old school we found for sale online. That's where we then built my current workshop. The space is efficient, bright, warm and very, very dusty. My view is of a beautiful valley surrounded by mountains and wildlife which inspires me constantly.

Do you travel from show to show? What are the best and worst aspects of life on the road? Feel free to share your most memorable story.

Although the opposite is the case for most artists, Mission Guild was Internet-born and later we started doing shows. There is nothing like seeing works of art in person and interacting with people face-to-face gives us valuable data to use in creating new work. I remember the first year we decided to do a show and decided to sleep over in the show trailer due to the lack of decent hotels in the area. I installed a shower in the cargo hold and we used an air mattress in the void where the cargo was. The nights were freezing and we quickly learned that we had to get up early to get ready and get out of that trailer because as soon as the sun came up, the trailer would heat up fast and cook us.

What is your attraction to the Roycroft arts community and the Roycrofters-At-Large Association? How has it impacted you as an artist?

The inspiration of our work comes from three places. First, the raw necessity of making a living; second, nature itself; and third, history of the craft, and that's were Roycroft comes in. A certain positive feeling comes from being part of this historic place in time. It gives fortitude to our intentions and let's us share in its relevance.

Where can people see and/or purchase your art?

Our principle venue is still our website, www.missionguild.com. We ship throughout the country and occasionally overseas to England, Japan, etc. Secondly, we participate in historically oriented shows like that of the Roycrofters-at-Large Association's summer and winter events. We also have our works available in a handful of gallery shops on the Roycroft Campus.

As an artist, what is the best piece of advice that you were ever given? What words of inspiration or advice would you offer those who might aspire to follow in your artistic footsteps?

All the advice I have ever heard about becoming an artist "as a living" has been dreadful, and for good reason. To be frank, creating art as a hobby or even therapy is valuable to the human sole, but art as a living is unbearably difficult to achieve. It will take a boatload of cash invested and/or a high-risk commitment. That being said, I must admit that it can be immensely gratifying as well.

Artists are, by nature, emotionally driven and seldom make good business owners, thus fail miserably often. Most artists I know do not rely on their art or craft for their living. Perhaps the pursuit of becoming an artist full time should be likened to many other small business ventures with a high rate of inherent danger of failing, like starting up a restaurant for example. The odds of success are poor and you will work absurd amounts of hours trying to stay afloat even if you are one of the few that survive.

On the bright side, there is no better feeling on earth than creating a special one-of-a-kind work of art that someone in the world actually loves enough to buy from you. So here is the quandary: On one hand you have high risk, on the other, great reward. What you do next can only happen if you are confident enough to accept either outcome willingly. Nothing ventured ...

Please share something else related to your craft which was not on this list of questions.

As a full-time artist, my goal and intentions may differ from the norm. I have already committed to the position everything that I am and my future depends largely on forward thinking and growth artistically. I am now in a stage of self-evolution that is born of my past but relies intensely on leaving it behind. Each new work that Christie and I create are flashes of energy that fuels the next one. To become better than before by observing our previous motions and the movements of our society around us takes precedents. It's our responsibility to contribute to the bettering of our world through art.

"If a man can write a better book, preach a better sermon, or make a better mousetrap than his neighbor, though he build his house in the woods, the world will make a beaten path to his door." — Ralph Waldo Emerson

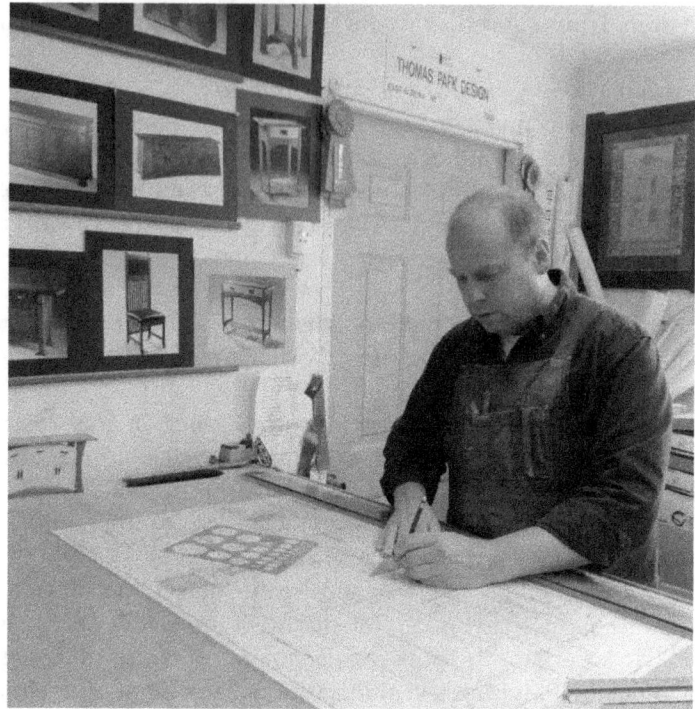

Describe your artistic specialty and what you typically like to create.

The media I work in is wood. For lack of a better way to put it, I'm a furniture maker and what I do is design and build custom furniture. I start by taking a concept from a client and then I sit down and do full drawings by hand. What I try to do in the niche that I fill is design and build one-of-a-kind custom pieces. They may be inspired by other historical designers, but the items I create tend to be a little more contemporary.

My goal has been, and continues to be, to design and build the highest quality furniture to suit a customer's specific needs. Each piece is created individually, taking as much time as necessary in the attempt to achieve perfection.

I look at the Arts and Crafts from 100 years ago and think how I can make it better and fit more with today's look. I like to call my work Arts and Crafts for the 21st century. I like to throw curves into each piece and use more exotic and unique materials. I also like to interject veneer into my pieces.

Describe the space where you typically create, and what is so special about that place?

I built the shop that I'm in now, which sits behind the Schoolhouse Gallery. I think I could have built it bigger, but hindsight is always twenty-twenty. It filled up pretty fast with materials and tools.

But I love working for myself and I love working in East Aurora. It's a great community, a community full of artists where there's always support and feedback.

Where can people see and/or purchase your art?

Many examples of my work can be seen and purchased at the Schoolhouse Gallery in East Aurora. You can also view my work on my website, www.thomaspafkdesign.com.

As an artist, what is the best piece of advice that you were ever given? What words of inspiration or advice would you offer those who might aspire to follow in your artistic footsteps?

I tell people who might be interested that this is not an easy craft to get into if you're going to do it professionally, one reason being that you have to buy high-quality tools. In this business, I barely survive. I barely make enough money to pay my bills. But the way I look at it is the tradeoff ... I get to do exactly what I want to do every day. It's what I love to do. I don't think you can buy happiness, but to come in here and make a decision about what I'm going to build that day — and use my tools to do it — that's the best job in the world! And the best part about my job is that I get to come in and do something different every day.

Please share something else related to your craft which was not on this list of questions.

You would think that I would run out of ideas after awhile but after nearly 30 years I've always been able to come up with new ideas. I have this creative thing inside of me that needs to get out. I get excited when someone comes in and they want to do something different and challenging, so it really is like creating art. When customers come in and ask me for a reproduction piece, I tell them that I can do something similar to that, but I can do it better and give them more of a unique design.

I definitely take a lot of pride in what I do and that's why I sign and date everything I create. I hope that long after I'm gone these pieces are going to be there and somebody might be refinishing the piece down the road and see who made it and where it was made. It's a sense of history and of leaving a legacy of something tangible. I always keep that in the back of my mind when I'm building a piece of furniture so that my best goes into it. I won't allow a piece to leave the shop unless it's to the best of my ability.

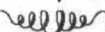

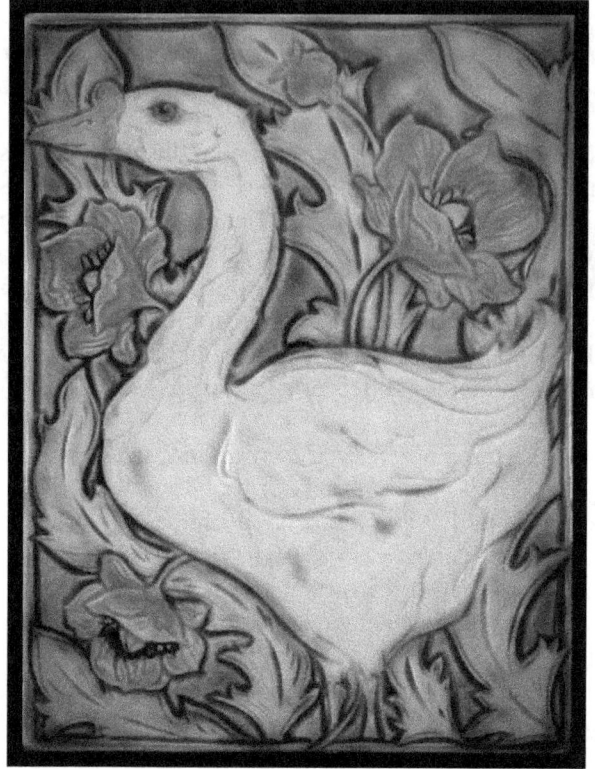

Describe your artistic specialty and what you typically like to create.

My work focus is in ceramics, predominantly as a tile maker, as well as vessels and sculpture.

I use a porcelaneous stoneware clay to produce my limited-production and custom-designed tiles, which are all hand-carved, pressed and hand-glazed with my own studio-designed glazes.

The sculptural work is made from various sculpture clay bodies, and surfaces are treated with various slips, engobes, stains and glazes, being fired multiple times.

Describe when you first truly realized that you had artistic skills, and how you worked to develop those skills.

Upon arriving at university, I chose to follow the path of art history, anthropology and archeology and left behind studio practice for a number of years. At the point of graduation I felt compelled to get my hands dirty, to start painting and making things again, and enrolled at Sheridan College School of Craft and Design.

Concentrating on ceramics, I fell in love with the possibilities of clay and have practiced ceramics full time in my production studio since then.

Since that time after completing my ceramics degree, I have done two artist residencies and have studied intensive MFA workshops at Alfred University and abroad. Getting away from a production studio — to challenge yourself and make something new — is a great opportunity which I hope I shall always be able to enjoy.

As an artist, what is the best piece of advice that you were ever given? What words of inspiration or advice would you offer those who might aspire to follow in your artistic footsteps?

Any words of advice, if asked, would be to follow your heart and make what you want to make. It is also very important to develop your business and marketing skills, and treat your work, however time-consuming, unique or specialized, as a business.

When someone looks at something you have created, what type of reaction or emotion do you hope to see, and why?

Often I find that people who see the tiles, or sculpture, create a narrative of their own for the imagery.

My work involves flora and fauna, and each have a story to tell, without sentimentality. Each person who takes a piece home has their own story or historical reference for it, whether it represents a loved one, their family or friends, or their thoughts on a moment in time.

Do you have an artistic goal — a bucket list project — that hasn't yet been met?

It is inherently important for an artist to continue always to grow in their work ... to refine their skills and to walk paths that they didn't expect and bring what they've learned back to their craft. This can happen when exploring new media, traveling or seeing something new. All your experiences inform your work and subtle changes occur over time.

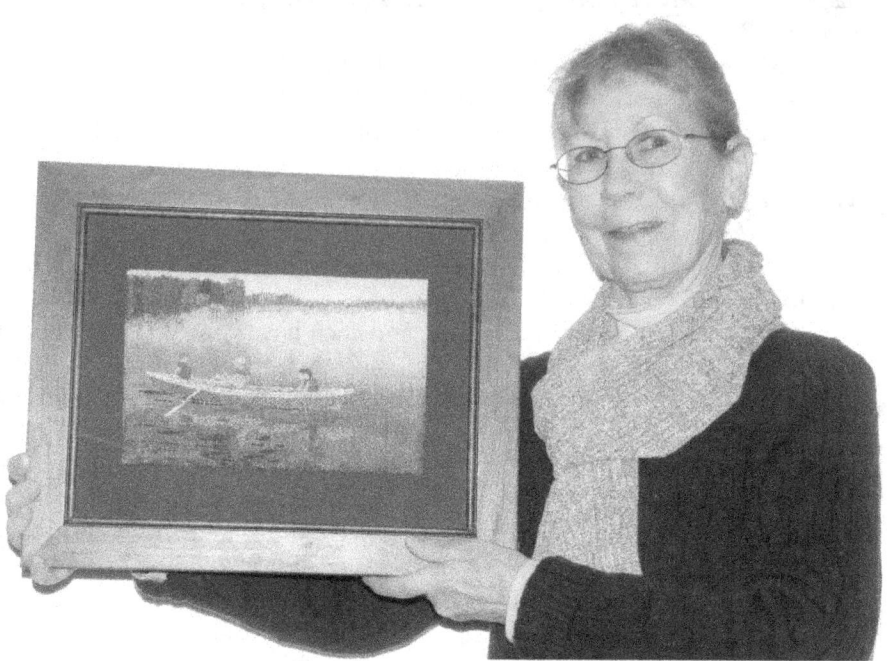

Describe your artistic specialty and what you typically like to create.

Hand weaving is my specialty. The fibers, yarn, fabrics, colors and tactile effects drew me toward the weaving craft. Whenever I dress the loom, I can imagine several additional possibilities and "what ifs." I do not focus on any type of cloth as I prefer to switch from type of yarn for fashions to home furnishings and to historical or contemporary fabrics. I seasonally demonstrate hand weaving with historical patterns and hand-dyed and hand-spun yarns at Genesee Country Village and Museum. The weaving products at the museum are used for some of the clothing and household furnishings.

At home I weave fabric for fashions, accessories and home furnishings. My favorite yarn is rayon chenille with its intense colors for the scarves and hats. The original designs are formulated in my mind, and then the yarns are chosen to produce a material which is sewn into the finished product. For home furnishing, I make small wall hangings, table runners, towels and rugs. During the winter I often weave commissioned historically styled rag rugs. I also develop "fiberscenes." The loom is dressed and the warp is painted. The weaving is done with sewing thread, selvedge to selvedge, alternated with textured heavier yarns to accentuate certain details in the landscape design. Once the cloth is off the loom, it is machine stitched, off tension, and hand stitched to complete the details.

Describe when you first truly realized that you had artistic skills, and how you worked to develop those skills.

As a young child I would make little drawings but I never considered myself as an "artist." In junior high school I quickly signed up for the wood shop as I felt it was far more interesting than cooking. In college, although my major was elementary education, I took many art courses (not to teach art). The courses included oil painting, watercolor painting, printmaking, interior/exterior home design, clay, wood, and several courses of drawing and composition classes. Textiles were not available at that time.

Years later I was sewing for family fashions and household needs. I couldn't find the exact color or texture of fabric that I wanted and the "artist" in me was greatly frustrated! I researched as to how cloth was made. Most weaving books of the time had poor instructions and a few fuzzy black-and-white photos. I found one book about rugs with precisely written details and explicit illustrations. I read the large book cover to cover and then I decided that I definitely wanted a floor loom!

With my first fabric weaving project, I couldn't wait until I could prepare for another "what if" project.

About a year later I met another weaver who encouraged me to join the Weavers' Guild. Although my knowledge of weaving primarily developed through reading and experimenting, I have also attended workshops for particular topics.

Who/what are your inspirations, and why?

Inspirations come everywhere and any time. Sometimes the end objective is known, but the development requires choosing the weave structure, fibers, colors and finishing. Other times I have no plan as to what the project will be. I have a large collection of yarns of different types and colors. Often I am inspirited by the textured yarns for specific weave structures.

Sometimes I see a design in stained glass or architectural details. Historical patterns and weave structures are often my sources. Watching people's activities or wearing a garment and in particular locations are inspiriting. I am forming a good composition in my mind as I see it.

The initial inspiration sometimes takes days or months or years to develop all the steps and details for the project before attending to the actual activity. I often work the development during routine household tasks. Often a yarn or color, despite samples prepared ahead of time, does not always work as hoped. Substitutes or redevelopments are sometimes changed during the working project.

Describe the space where you typically create, and what is so special about that place?

Creating in natural light is my preference, although the addition of artificial light eliminates shadows. I have a room off the kitchen for my 12-harness loom and a cabinet sewing machine with two large windows. The room is the primary work space, convenient to the kitchen but not near enough space for my looms, equipment, related books and yarns.

An antique barn frame loom (a garage sale discard) is squeezed into one side of the enclosed porch (three walls of windows). My first purchased floor loom is tucked into one corner of the living room with a large window. The most recent small portable floor loom is taken to workshops and our seasonal place. Two later 19th century looms are stored (so they won't be scraped) in the basement. My first loom was a metal frame to make potholders and I still use it when needed. That and the remainder of the tabletop looms are stored until needed. A former bedroom is home for books and yarns. Two good sized windows are perfect for yarn and weave structure selections. It is a quiet room for creative time.

Please share something else related to your craft which was not on this list of questions.

I like to bounce from century to century. The changes from one century to the next involve major textile changes.

In Western New York, at the end of the 18th century and the beginning of the 19th century, it was a time of self sufficiency in textile processes. With better transportation, machine-made cotton yarns and fabric became available. Those changes can be seen at Genesee Country Village and Museum. I enjoy demonstrating and having the opportunity to explain the related textile history to visitors.

Toward the end of 19th century and the beginning of the 20th century, people were realizing that not all machine-made items were always the best. There was a renaissance and the appreciation of the handmade craftsman efforts, such as the Roycroft, came into vogue. I also enjoy making handmade hand-woven items and hope that others appreciate the quality craftsman's efforts.

Now in the beginning of the 21st century, we have greater techniques for treating yarns and new fibers. As a weaver, I combine the use of the 19th century patterns with 20th century renaissance appreciation and 21st century fiber technology.

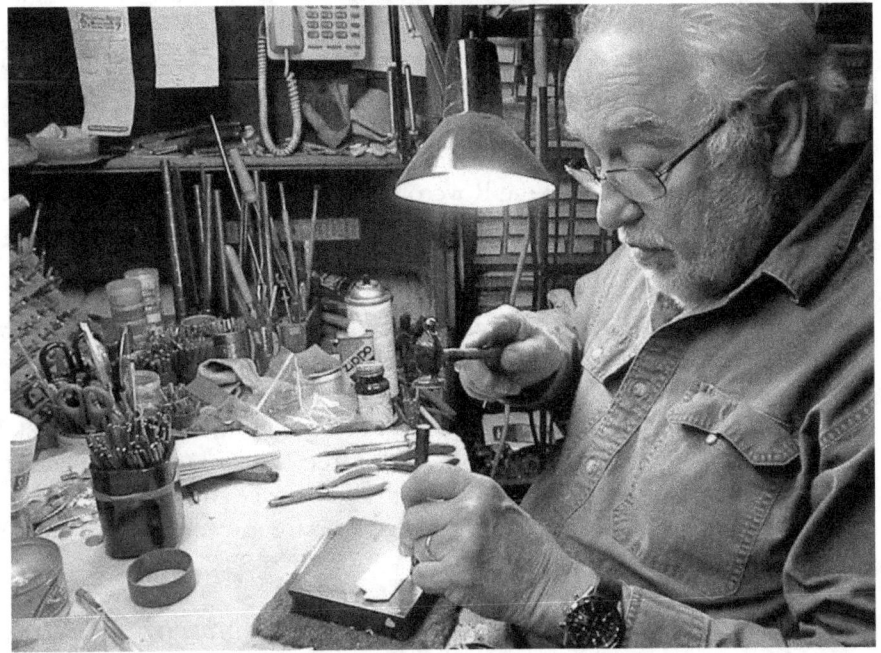

Describe your artistic specialty and what you typically like to create.

I am a jeweler that specializes in Arts and Crafts-style chasing. I like to create jewelry and other metal objects that have a Roycroft flavor and style.

I began to work with metal in high school metal shop class. I had a very good teacher who encouraged me to experiment. He also taught me how to make chasing tools and heat treat them properly so as to last a lifetime. By the time I graduated from high school I had a mixed assortment of chasing tools that I had made and began practicing and developing some skill in the chasing process.

Who/what are your inspirations, and why?

I have always been inspired by the work of Walter Jennings, the former superintendent of the Roycroft Copper Shop. I was fortunate to have met him in his studio as a young college student where he taught me how to make the square tudor rose. He told me to go home and make my own tools and practice. I took that as a challenge and permission to incorporate the tudor rose on my work.

Describe the space where you typically create, and what is so special about that place?

My studio space is in the basement of my home which allows me to go there any time for as long as I like. This allows me to develop areas for special processes and operations.

What is your attraction to the Roycroft arts community and the Roycrofters-At-Large Association? How has it impacted you as an artist?

In 1976 I was asked by the newly created Roycrofters-At-Large Association to represent the organization as a working artisan. I was encouraged to use the new double "R" mark on my work. I have used that mark for nearly 40 years and I'm still proud to use it every time I strike it into my work. I am even prouder today to be a Master Artisan because the organization is blessed to have the finest craftsmen and women who are working with their highly developed skills. The organization has a well established process of selection for inviting new artisans into the organization and allowing them to use the Roycroft mark on their work.

Where can people see and/or purchase your art?

I am currently selling at the Roycroft Copper Shop, the Roycroft Artisans Gallery on Olean Road in East Aurora, and on the Fair Oaks Workshop web page in Chicago.

As an artist, what is the best piece of advice that you were ever given? What words of inspiration or advice would you offer those who might aspire to follow in your artistic footsteps?

Make your own tools, and practice. Find a master metalsmith and ask for an apprenticeship, even if you have to work for free. Try not to give up your regular employment and try to develop your own studio space so as to continue your own work. Remember that Roycrofter-At-Large Artisans are good sources of help and encouragement.

When someone looks at something you have created, what type of reaction or emotion do you hope to see, and why?

I want them to look at my work and have an appreciation for the effort involved in its creation. I want them to see the beauty in the workmanship and in the design of the piece. The emotion I want to see is that this piece is handmade, here in East Aurora, by one of a limited number of artisans that can do this work. And that with reasonable care, it will be passed down through generations.

As an artist, what has been your most significant achievement, or proudest moment, to date?

There have been many moments. One of the best was to be invited to do the Disney show in Florida. In order to be selected one has to take a Best of Show Award at a nationally recognized craft show.

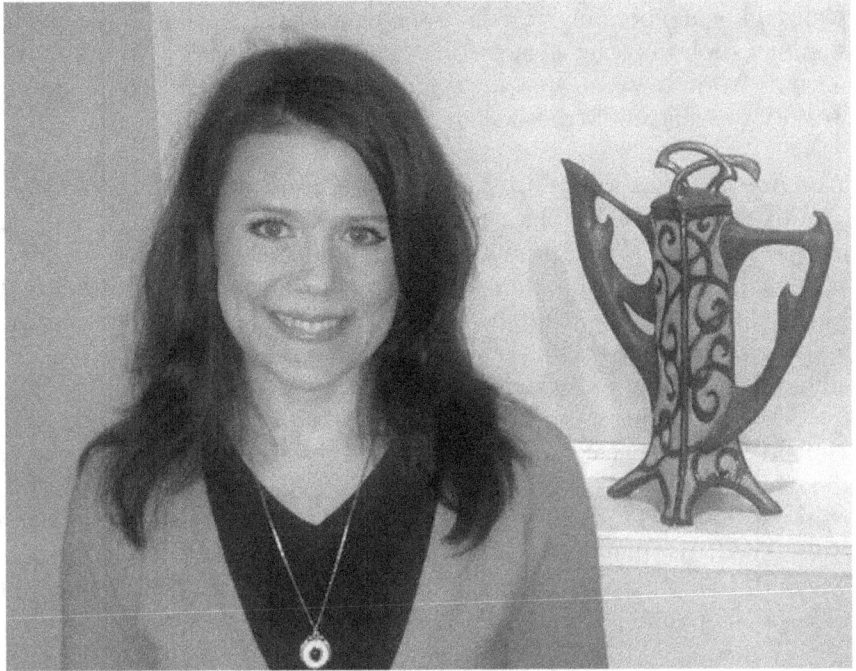

Describe your artistic specialty and what you typically like to create.

I am a ceramic artist. The work that I create differs from what many people would traditionally call ceramics in that I design and construct teapots, vessels, boxes, etc. with a strong sculptural element to them. The sculptural element can be translated in my instance by explaining that they are technically functional but the bodies are heavily carved and handles are ornately curved and twisted. Time-consuming and minutely carved areas are added, and patinas, glazes and lusters are fused during repeated firings. I enjoy the time-consuming, intricate and beauty centered nature of the style of ceramics I have chosen to pursue.

Who/what are your inspirations, and why?

I have always loved the natural world. I am a detail-oriented person. I also have always had a strong link to family and the connection that families have to precious objects passed down from generations. These things might include something as simple as a kitchen tool or a rusty iron garden clipper, or as precious as a piece of jewelry. This mix has led me to the sensibilities of the Art Nouveau movement, a strong influence in my work even today.

The inspiration, however, that catches me off guard the most are everyday things I see and touch ... the shape and texture of an old aluminum tray, a pod from a plant, a leaf that has dried and rotted to leave just the skeleton of veins, dragonflies, beets in the summer garden.

That all being said, my favorite inspiration and what has been the most influential to my work was a visit to the Art Nouveau show at the National Gallery in Washington, D.C., about 14 years ago. I saw a beautiful leather book cover with fall leaves carved into the surface. I had at that point already been heavily carving my artwork, which is why I think the book held such an attraction. I began to think about the fact that at a point, clay becomes similar to leather during its drying process. I realized I would not only be able to carve the clay, I could also use tiny leather stamping tools to create an additional layer of visual interest/texture to my already intricate work. It was an amazing revelation to me that changed everything about my work. It was a lightbulb moment.

Describe the space where you typically create, and what is so special about that place?

My greatest wish is to have a studio someday that is above ground with a door that opens outside so, in the summer, I could wander around in my bare feet and make pots on the wheel looking at the garden. But that isn't the way it is; the studio my husband and I share is in the basement. When we bought our little house 12 years ago, the room to the back of our basement was the exact space we needed for a studio. It was a sign for sure.

My husband Jerry and I have always worked in a basement studio, from the Buffalo State College ceramics program where we met, to now. Jerry has always been the really special thing about those spaces. When we are in our studio together working, it is filled with creative energy. It is the people in the space that make it work. We have often discussed the possibility of that being a "clay" artist thing. The wonderful gift of having someone to help you when you are struggling with a design or lifting a 100-pound ceramic sculpture into the kiln is priceless.

What is your attraction to the Roycroft arts community and the Roycrofters-At-Large Association? How has it impacted you as an artist?

When I was in high school, my art teacher told us about the Arts and Crafts Movement, Frank Lloyd Wright and Roycroft, and I was hooked. The concept of making and having beautiful artwork that you would use every day was an absolute draw. I think back now and in reality it was pieces fitting together; the parts assembled becoming obvious to what they related to and represented.

I had always treasured those unique, well-made old items passed down through the generations. The house I grew up in, built in 1886 that my parents restored — hardwood floors, carved wooden mantel, wrought and cast iron everywhere — introduced me to the idea of beauty in design and craftsmanship. It gave me a sense of living someplace that was special because of the thought, time and effort skilled hands had created. I didn't know what it was called but I appreciated it all, even then.

Hearing what the Roycroft was about, what it did, its philosophy and its elite status pulled all of those former life experiences into focus and created the desire to be a part of a group that was like-minded. I am completely a part of that old school, perfectionistic, hands-on sense of a hard day's work to create functional beauty.

As an artist, what has been your most significant achievement, or proudest moment, to date?

I had my work accepted into the Strictly Functional Pottery National at a gallery in Eastern Pennsylvania. The juror of the show was Ken Ferguson, an amazing ceramics professor and artist from Kansas City. The piece that was accepted was my first really "major piece." It was a teapot that was covered in ginkgo leaves, beginnings of my intricate design. Arranging to get to the opening proved tricky, but my parents picked me up from work, drove with me the six hours and we made it just in time. I changed my clothes in the car. The spring weather was beautiful as we walked into the show. I saw my piece, a red dot and an award plaque! I had won the award for innovation AND sold my piece!

Ken Ferguson was there and I spoke with him for a few moments. He was gracious, giving me bits of advice: Work with even more intricacy, more detail, continue on my path.

I think about that night often. It was the most incredible feeling to have my parents there to celebrate my first major victory. We were all so elated and floating on a high of happiness, success and pride. I felt so blessed.

It was a gift to speak with Ken Ferguson. Ken passed away not long after the show. My father has passed since then.

That night wasn't the last time I won an award or sold a big piece. It was the preciousness of the moment and the people that meant so much. It seemed like magic.

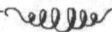

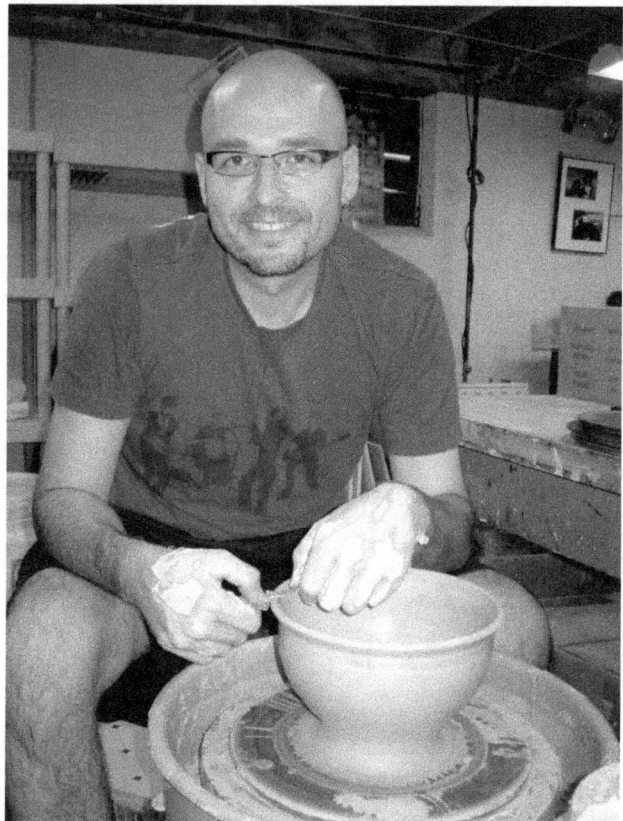

Describe your artistic specialty and what you typically like to create.

I am a ceramic (clay) artist and typically like to produce thrown, altered and assembled functional pottery, as well as nautical and mechanical themed contemplative sculpture and wall pieces.

My wheel focus looks to creating tableware that combines both form and function, spanning classical to the contemporary. Applying a sculptor's mind to round wheel thrown forms most often leads to asymmetrical stretched and visually dynamic pots. Two or more glazes are sprayed in combination to accentuate the visual movements and lines of the physical form.

Sculptural pieces are a narrative on my personal observations and focus on elevating and preserving obsolete mechanical objects from the past. Living and working in Buffalo, New York, has inspired many pieces detailing the city's architecture, forgotten steel mills and waterfront industries, as well as its Great Lakes shipping and maritime history. Finishing the sculptures in varying patinas and decaying metallic glazes helps to promote that element of time passing away.

Describe when you first truly realized that you had artistic skills, and how you worked to develop those skills.

My sixth grade art teacher from Marcy (New York) Elementary, Mr. Ashcroft, invited me and a few others to join an art club after school a few days a week. After a year of doing more advanced projects than that of a typical grade school student, using materials such as sheet metal and rivets, wood for carving and modeling wax for casting, our time together was coming to a close. On one of the final days in that building, I was pulled from my regular class and asked to join Mr. Ashcroft for a special project. Together we went outside and to my surprise I helped him plant a small sapling tree.

That afternoon while digging a hole out in the school's courtyard I was told that I had some artistic talent and that I should continue to develop my skills as I moved onto middle and later high school. He told me that he was very proud of the work I was doing and that he expected to hear good things about me in the future. I went on to study art and all of the electives I could to better myself as a young artist.

Reflecting back on those early days, I see that I was given the confidence to find my "visual voice" as an artist, although it would take many more such encounters with other wonderful teachers and professors before I would actually allow myself to speak out loud to the public.

Who/what are your inspirations, and why?

My summer vacations were spent helping my retired grandfather, Gerald Sr., fix up my grandparent's home and to keep their antique-looking 1960's car running. "Pop" built the home after returning from WWII before starting a successful auto repair business that would employ all of his children, including me at the early age of eight.

One summer vacation project was to encase the exterior window sills on the house in aluminum flashing. We measured, scored, cut and hand bent the aluminum all day, going from window to window until late in the evening. I spent most of the time watching and taking long breaks to play with my beat up remote-controlled car.

The next day I thought I was in for another round of windows, but Pop had a different plan. We sculpted a new sheet metal body for my little R/C car. What a craftsman! He did things with a metal sheet and some hand tools that I could not comprehend; every detail fashioned into that beautiful shiny new car body. He never admitted that he was an artist, he would just say that he liked to make stuff function and make it function well.

His friendship, his humor and his lessons on life and how it related to auto repair, and his unconditional love of all whom he met, still inspire me today. He helped me to understand that working with your hands, as well as your creative mind, can make the most imaginative thoughts into reality.

Do you have an artistic goal — a bucket list project — that hasn't yet been met?

My perfect piece or project is to combine ceramic sculpture and tile permanently into several architectural elements of our home. We remodeled a few years back and placed ceramic tile backer board in several locations. The list includes a dimensional front door surround, entryway floor and wall tiles, a floor-to-ceiling fireplace surround including the mantle, and several tile projects in the kitchen. The kitchen tiles have been planned and started, but the other areas will need more thought and problem solving before they come to fruition.

The hardest part of interior design is coming to grips with living inside of those design choices for quite a few years. Unlike smaller pieces that can be moved or stored out of sight when they seem dated, these design choices need to be timeless!

The house would become a piece unto itself. Taking the utilitarian characteristics of functional ceramics and combining them with the deeper meaning of thought-provoking sculpture will be a process ... a process that will marry craft and (fine) art together.

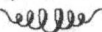
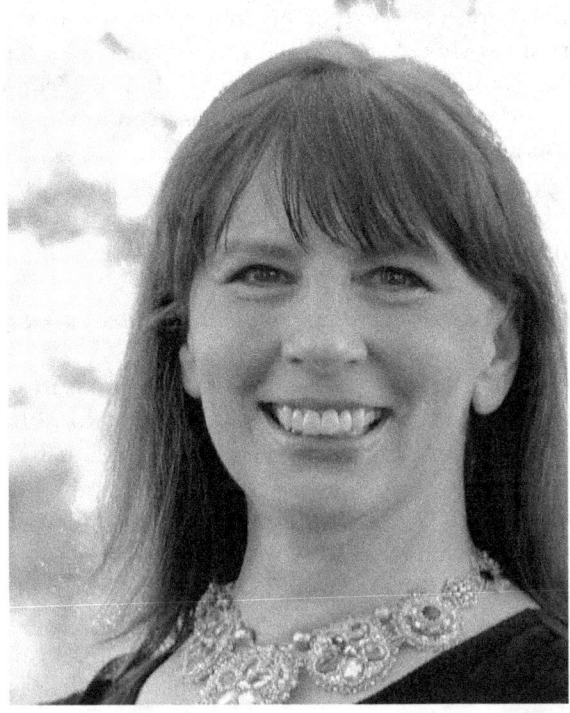

Describe your artistic specialty and what you typically like to create.

I work with beads of all kinds to make jewelry, but mostly with tiny glass seed beads. I create jewelry of all sizes from small pendants to large intricate beaded collars.

Who/what are your inspirations, and why?

This is hard to pin down. I draw great inspiration from different components. Stone cabochons, broken bits of old jewelry, just about anything. I have worked many different unusual components into my beadwork, including butterfly wings, fossils, unpolished rocks and feathers. I draw the colors and feelings from these components and work from there.

When I am stuck and need some inspiration I usually look at books of old Native American work, vintage jewelry, paintings, textiles or just nature. It is amazing the textures and colors you can find when you are paying attention to the nature around you!

I have visited many Native American museums. The intricate and exacting work never fails to humble and inspire me. Seeing how these items have survived to this day inspires me to pay particular attention to my workmanship and to make it so it lasts. I want to create jewelry that can be handed down from generation to generation.

Where can people see and/or purchase your art?

I have work for sale at the Copper Shop on the Roycroft Campus. It has been difficult to keep up inventory since my pieces are so labor intensive, so there is only a limited amount there. I also exhibit at a number of art shows in the Northeastern U.S.

Exhibiting at art shows, particularly outdoor shows, is very challenging physically ... and sometimes mentally as well! So recently I have become more involved with teaching beadwork throughout the U.S. It has been fun to meet people from all around the country who are interested in working with beads, and hopefully I have inspired a few to pursue this creative outlet. I write tutorials for specific pieces of beadwork and sell these along with kits online in my Etsy shop. My website is www.bettystephan.com.

When someone looks at something you have created, what type of reaction or emotion do you hope to see, and why?

Sometimes at an art show, a person comes in and is in such awe and joy when looking at my work. That is the feeling I would hope for. I have felt that way looking that others' work. The feeling just floods over me in a rush and I want to touch it and just soak it in.

I want people to look past the "how long did that take" and the technicalities of the piece and just get that feeling of awe and joy. Those other questions come after. I guess the short answer is that I would like my viewers to feel something when they look at it. Not just see it as a technical piece of work.

Something that creates this feeling is not something I can plan. I don't know how it happens exactly, I think it has to come through your hands from your heart.

As an artist, what has been your most significant achievement, or proudest moment, to date?

I think my most exciting achievement was when my piece "Cathedral Windows" was featured on the cover of the book "500 Beaded Jewelry." I still get a thrill when I happen to run across it at a bookstore. I was also one of 30 bead artists chosen to be included in the book "Marcia DeCoster Presents." These artists were chosen from all over the world, so it was quite an honor. My extended interview was published in this book, as well as many pictures of my beaded necklaces.

Other significant and exciting achievements include receiving the Award of Excellence at the Chautauqua Crafts Alliance show in 2014, being accepted as a Roycroft Master Artisan in 2013, and being juried into the Burchfield Penney Art in Craft show.

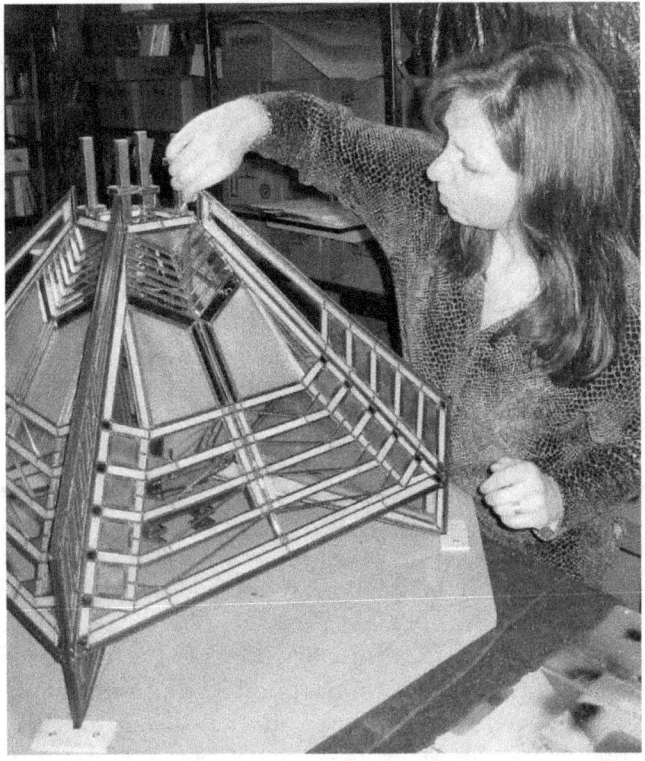

Describe your artistic specialty and what you typically like to create.

My artistic specialty is glass, and what I typically create is anything in stained glass such as lamps, jewelry boxes and windows. I also do fused glass, and paint on the glass with powdered glass and add shards of glass for texture. I will often incorporate nature scenes into my work. I do fused glass jewelry also, and with the jewelry I incorporate crystal, which is leaded glass.

Describe when you first truly realized that you had artistic skills, and how you worked to develop those skills.

Ever since I was a little kid I loved to make things with my hands. Any material I could get my hands on, I would make something out of it. I did origami and I also learned how to knit when I was just around 5 years old. I broke my collarbone when I was 8 and I taught myself to crochet; I crocheted a whole poncho back then. I would make jewelry as a kid, and I also did string art and sewing.

In school I was always good in math and art, so when I went to college I wanted to combine those two things and I thought interior design or fashion design might be a good fit. With fashion design I thought I'd have to live in Paris or New York City my whole life to have a career, but I thought with interior design I could live anywhere that I wanted. I guess I didn't want to stray too far from the Buffalo area.

However, I did end up going to the Fashion Institute of Technology in New York City for two years, but then I thought I wanted to study architecture. I decided to work and go back to school at night for my bachelor's degree, and then I wanted to get my master's degree. By that time I was married for a number of years and pregnant with my son. I finished my master's when he was one. I received both my bachelor's and master's degree in architecture from UB (University at Buffalo).

When I eventually went back to work I worked at Cannon Design as an interior architect. I wasn't making that much money compared to when I was an interior designer working for General Motors in their facilities planning department. My daughter, our second child, was born, and rather than put two kids into daycare my husband and I decided that I would stay home and take care of them. In my heart I could not leave them. With that I started to take a night class at UB in their creative craft center and I took a stained glass class, and once I took it I was hooked. I took two classes and then I just taught myself the rest and never stopped doing stained glass.

So that's how the whole thing started. It's kind of funny how your life changes direction, and in this case it was all for the best. I feel very blessed that I can work with my hands and be happy at it. And that's what I teach my kids, too ... do whatever is in your heart and be happy.

Describe the space where you typically create, and what is so special about that place?

I work out of my basement as that's where my studio is currently located, but there are different parts of stained glass that I only do in certain areas. When I cut glass, for example, I only cut in one part of the basement, and when I solder there's another area that I solder in. Soldering is the most time-consuming part of doing stained glass. Sometimes when I do the copper foil method I take pieces of cut ground glass and put the copper foil around it as I'm sitting in front of the TV, or when my husband is driving and we're on a long drive I might bring it along with me and work on it in the car. My work — the foiling part of it — is portable, so some days I'll just bring it outside and work on the deck.

Eventually I will be renting a studio in the Print Building on the Roycroft Campus. I'm going to be moving part of my home studio and working daytime hours there. It will be nice having two studio spaces.

What is your attraction to the Roycroft arts community and the Roycrofters-At-Large Association? How has it impacted you as an artist?

What attracted me to the Roycroft community was first studying interior design. I loved the Arts and Crafts movement, even back then. I was drawn to William Morris and John Ruskin, the founders of the Arts and Crafts Movement in England. Arts and Crafts incorporates a lot of the arts, and the whole idea of quality and hand craftsmanship was why I was drawn to it.

Living in this area I was always drawn to the Roycroft Campus. One day, I think In 2005 when the Copper Shop was first opened under the Roycroft Campus Corporation, I was driving by and I stopped in to look around. I was always inspired by the different artists' work that Kitty Turgeon had in there, but this time it was all new and right from day one I started bringing in things to sell in the Copper Shop. The next step for me was to become a Roycroft Artisan and become more a part of the Roycroft community.

I love being exposed to everyone else's designs, and that inspires me to do more in the Arts and Crafts style, even though I like to do contemporary things too.

As an artist, what is the best piece of advice that you were ever given? What words of inspiration or advice would you offer those who might aspire to follow in your artistic footsteps?

The best piece of advice I was ever given was from one of my professors at UB who was actually a working architect who told me to always strive for museum quality. It's tough, but it pushes you to achieve something that might be hard to achieve.

As for a piece of advice I would give to others, it would be to always follow your heart. That applies to anything in life.

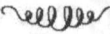
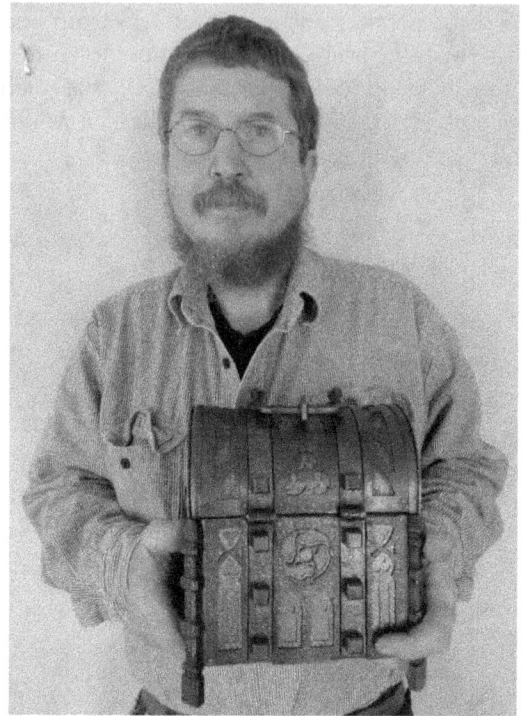

Describe your artistic specialty and what you typically like to create.

I started blacksmithing in 1985 with a focus on making swords and woodworking chisels. In the thirty years that I have been a blacksmith I have yet to start a sword and have started a few woodworking chisels but have not finished them. I know how to make both the swords and chisels but I found myself taking different paths.

I started to focus on copper in about 1990. I made flowers out of copper as well as garden sculptures such as frogs, lizards, butterflies, bats, etc. to place in the yard. As the Internet continued to come online I decided that I could not sell my garden sculpture over the Internet as the shipping would more than double the price, making them too expensive. So I started to make copper boxes. It was at this time that I discovered the Roycrofters and their fine copper work.

I was not able to find anyone teaching this style so I started to teach myself by studying all the books I could find on the Roycrofters. Robert Trout started to teach this style of work at John C. Campbell Folk School in Murphy, North Carolina. I took his first two classes in 2003 and 2004. These classes taught me the important elements of the Roycroft style as well as the types of chisel for this style of work. From that point on I have continued to teach myself, progressing from Roycroft Artisan to Master.

Describe the space where you typically create, and what is so special about that place?

My studio is in the back of a working rock quarry inside an old cast iron foundry that was shut down because of the Clean Air Act in 1971. As many artist do for inexpensive studio space, I have a 6,000-square-foot shop but no running water. The space is very organic as many buildings around me are being reclaimed by nature with vegetation overgrowing and the wind tearing it apart.

Do you travel from show to show? What are the best and worst aspects of life on the road? Feel free to share your most memorable story.

I do thirty shows a year in a twelve-hour radius of Birmingham, from as far away as Dallas-Fort Worth to Reston, Virginia, to St. Petersburg, Florida. I also teach at least four weeks a year. I enjoy meeting and interacting with the people who buy my work. Not meeting with the collectors is a downside to selling work in a gallery. I do sell at the River Gallery in Chattanooga, Tennessee, but I do demonstrate at the gallery so I can meet with collectors.

What is your attraction to the Roycroft arts community and the Roycrofters-At-Large Association? How has it impacted you as an artist?

The Roycrofters inspire me to do the best work that I can possibly do in the spirit of maintaining the quality of the Roycroft craftsmen that came before me.

Where can people see and/or purchase your art?

My work is available at the River Gallery in Chattanooga, Tennessee. I do have a good website which is roberttaylormetalsmith.com. By going to as many as thirty shows a year I am able to promote my website. When people come to shows they might be ready to buy at that time, and because I have my pieces there to inspect for quality they have greater confidence to buy my work. There is no substitute for holding a piece in your hands.

As an artist, what is the best piece of advice that you were ever given? What words of inspiration or advice would you offer those who might aspire to follow in your artistic footsteps?

The best advice is to do your best, push the limits of your ability, never stop learning and remember that as you continue to strive for perfection you will find that it turns out to be a moving target. Also, as people helped teach you, you should pay it forward and teach others without restrictions.

When someone looks at something you have created, what type of reaction or emotion do you hope to see, and why?

I want people to recognize the quality of my work and the amount of effort and dedication that I take to complete the piece.

Do you have an artistic goal — a bucket list project — that hasn't yet been met?

The bucket list would include learning how to make a fine quality conical-shaped lampshade by capturing the wire in the rim. Also, I would like to learn how to make a dovetail seam that would join sheet copper, giving me the option to make bowls and vases.

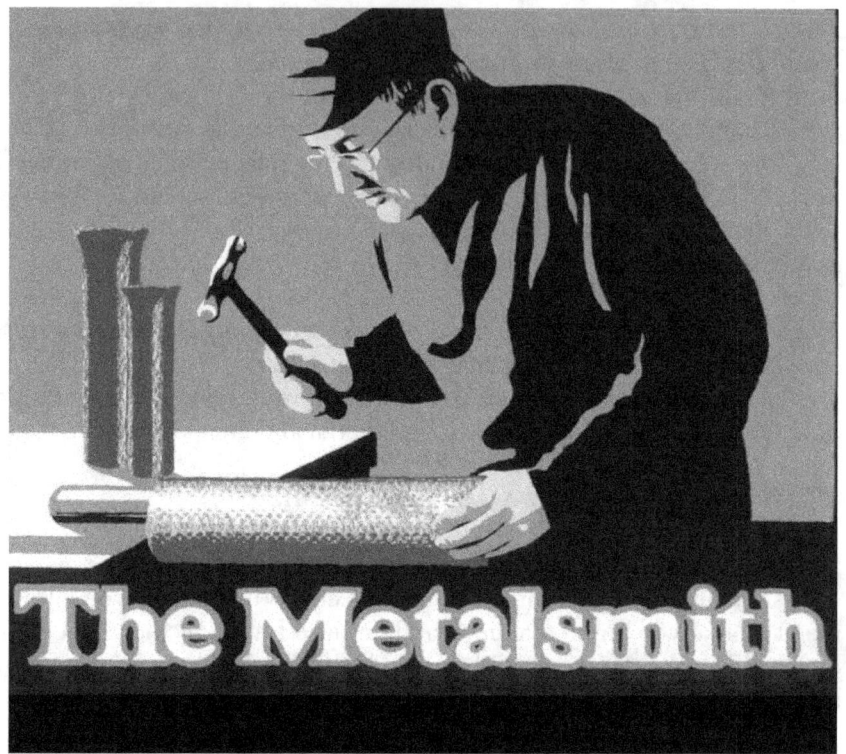

Describe your artistic specialty and what you typically like to create.

I work in metal, and lots of copper. I also work in fine wrought iron for the pure joy of it.

Describe when you first truly realized that you had artistic skills, and how you worked to develop those skills.

When I was around 8 or 10 years old I knew I wanted to work with my hands. When I was around that same age there was a posting in the newspaper that said, "Can you draw me?" It was a Dick Tracy profile, and I could. Move ahead a few years and my aunt told me about a summer program at the art gallery for a free art class for the summer. I signed up for it and I liked it! Later on I was given a scholarship for art when I was around 13 or 14.

My art took a break for awhile. In 1969 I was accepted into an apprenticeship for skilled trades as a sheet metal welder. For me this was working with my hands and I was able to make a good living. Four years later I was what you would call a "B" journeyman at the Xerox Corp in the in-plant group.

Fast forward to 1979 when my wife and I were in Mystic Seaport, Connecticut, visiting the ship smith shop where the smith told me about a group that met once a year for blacksmithing. I went to that meeting near Kingston, New York, in the fall and I was gone — hook, line and sinker — for blacksmithing.

For the next 25 years or so I was a blacksmith and liked it. In the plant I was working 65 hours a week or more for over 10 years, and I was looking for a break.

That's when I started working with copper, and I liked it. At the time when I juried for the mark in 1999, the company was offering training at any level and I took a course at RIT and it was life-changing for me, night and day for my level of work. By 2000 I took early retirement at the age of 57 and never looked back.

Now I am a mentor and teacher in the craft of copper and I study fine wrought iron (1500s Germany) and love the work. It's gothic in form and for me very detailed and fun to do.

At age 72, I at long last find joy in my work and great joy in helping others in their quest in metal, whether it's copper or wrought iron.

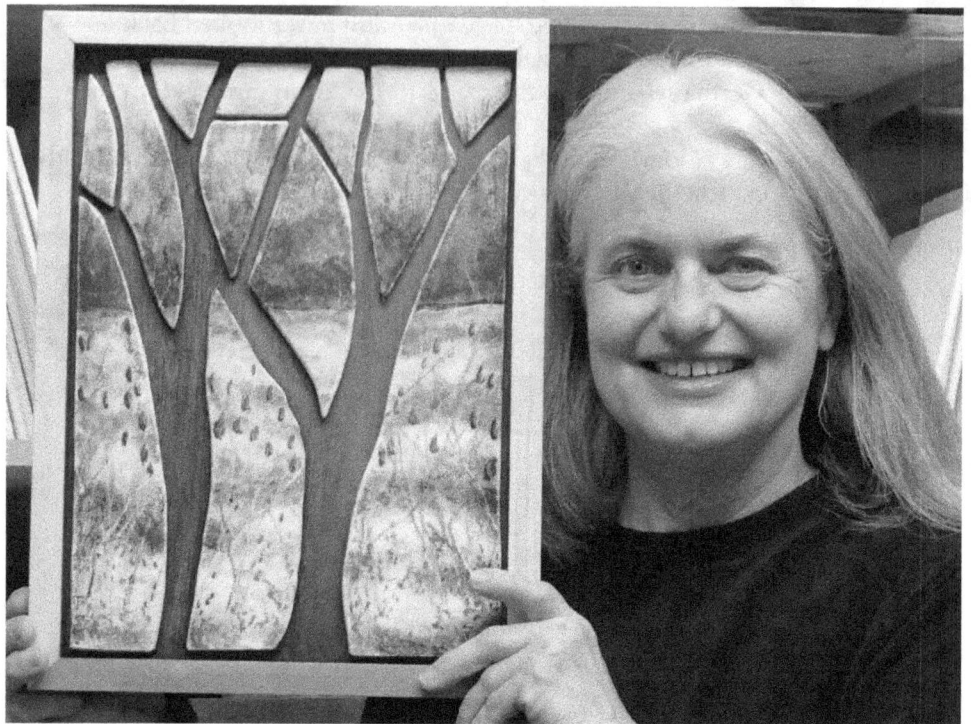

Describe your artistic specialty and what you typically like to create.

I work with clay. Clay starts out as a pliable, damp lump, but once fired it becomes solid, strong and vitreous. I enjoy working with clay equally because of the varied methods of construction and the magic of the firing.

For years I worked as a studio potter. I used the potter's wheel to create symmetrical, functional pottery for everyday use. I enjoyed the repetitive wedging of the clay and the centering on the wheel, making a Zen-like focus. I finished my pots by painting floral designs with stains and oxides, mixed in water, directly on the raw glaze similar to watercolor. The work is fired to 2,200 degrees causing the glaze to melt and the colors to shift a bit creating an impressionistic look.

My painting became more elaborate, so I started to make tiles instead of pots to paint on. They could be put on the wall instead of hidden in a cupboard. With tiles I could make larger scale work and this appealed to me.

To make tiles, I still work with wet clay. I roll it into sheets, cut the shapes, and then dry them slowly between sheetrock to keep the tiles from warping. Once dried and fired to bisque, I glaze them and paint with my stain-water mix.

Recently, I am working with rustic, textural sculptures of natural forms. Instead of the fine finish and symmetry of the potter's wheel, I am using my hands as the main tool. I am inspired by stacked stones and how they silhouette against the sky.

I am also experimenting with raku firing, a much more spontaneous and unpredictable firing technique. The clay pieces are fired in a gas kiln and heated to 1,300 to 1,800 degrees, depending on what I want to achieve. Once the temperature is reached, they are removed from the heat and placed into a can with combustibles.

The hot pot ignites the materials, then I close the lid to cut off the supply of oxygen. The fire smolders and the smoke penetrates the piece.

Working with clay never gets old. There is always more to learn and experience.

Describe when you first truly realized that you had artistic skills, and how you worked to develop those skills.

I can't remember a time when I was not interested in art. My grandmother painted large florals in oil. She used many layers of leaves and ferns pressed with shades of greens in the background for her flower arrangements. I poured over books illustrated with Hudson Valley and early American paintings. Illustrations told the stories.

Even though my teachers would give me the job of decorating the bulletin board or designing the class art project, I knew I wanted to get better and "become" an artist.

As a Girl Scout I was lucky to be able to visit artist and potters' studios, the art museum, and work on art badges. I spent a summer in Virginia's Appalachian Mountains, immersed in folk art. That was my first experience on the potter's wheel.

I studied art at the University of New Mexico and the University of North Florida with a concentration on ceramics. My real education began once I was working full time as a studio potter. Spending the time with clay in my studio, trial and error and practice; getting the feel of the clay and learning what the clay will do was the real teacher.

I read articles in Ceramics Monthly, Studio Potter and any magazines I could get my hands on. I belonged to art organizations and co-ops, and would share ideas and information with other potters. I would visit museums and exhibitions as often as possible.

I have learned after all these years that maybe one does not "become" and artist, but just is an artist.

Do you travel from show to show? What are the best and worst aspects of life on the road? Feel free to share your most memorable story.

For the past 40 years I have made a living by selling my clay work. This has mostly been done on the road, going from show to show. I started out showing locally in Florida. After a few years, I started showing in the Northeast during the hot summer months. To do this I had to make lots of work, buy a trailer, pack up the work and spend time on the road. As a potter, it is hard to be away from the studio for too long. I could not make clay work while traveling. I could only do two to four shows then had to return to the studio.

This gypsy lifestyle is not all fun and games as most people think. I have had many people say to me, "What a fun life you must have." They don't realize the expense, travel and work this takes. This involves packing up and hauling the work; setting up a booth at odd hours of the morning or night with tent, lights and display stands; being on your feet all day in all kinds of weather; smiling and explaining your work for two to four days in a row and then packing up and moving on for the next weekend. It is exhausting.

So I go on with this season after season, and year after year. Why? There is something great about seeing all of my work displayed. Once I am surrounded by it, I can really see it and think, "Wow, I love this." I also love to share my work with interested customers. I enjoy making a connection and explaining my work and what inspires me.

I've made so many friends with other artist and craftspeople. By sharing this crazy life, we become almost a family.

Where can people see and/or purchase your art?

I still travel to art shows but keep closer to home. I show mostly in Western New York but I do travel to parts of New England. Some of these shows include 100 American Craftsmen in Lockport, New York; the Roycroft shows in East Aurora, New York; Clothesline in Rochester, New York; Arts in the Garden, Sonnenburg Gardens, Canandaigua, New York; Colorscape in Norwich, New York; The Artrider Show at Lyndhurst Castle in Tarrytown, New York; and the Craft Alliance Show at the Chautauqua Institute in Mayville, New York.

I also do a show at my studio with the Allegany Artisans every October, the weekend after Columbus Day. This is the time I open my studio to the public to display my work for sale and demonstrate my working with clay. I have been a part of this show for the past 21 years. It has developed into a great show and a fun weekend.

This spring I am a visiting artist at the Cazenovia Artisans Gallery and the Power House on the Roycroft Campus.

My work is sold at the Canacadea Country Store in Alfred, Mostly Clay in Pittsford, The Little Gem in Wellsville, and the Copper Shop in East Aurora.

As an artist, what has been your most significant achievement, or proudest moment, to date?

The most satisfying and exciting accomplishment of my career was the first public art installation that I was commissioned to do. Our town built a new library and granted money for art. I was selected to make and install a mural for the exterior above the door. This was quite a project and challenged me with many details. I had to plan for the shrinkage of the clay for a specific space and make sure the clay would hold up in this weather. I wanted the design to relate to the area and be appreciated by the public.

This project led to many more public art grants and commissions, including working with the town's people to make a "tile community quilt." I organized workshops so that each person could paint their own 4x4 tile. There are more than 400 tiles that line the interior walls of this library.

A school commissioned me to design its logo and a tile image of that logo for the school's entryway. Another community arts grant was awarded me to work with art students to help design a mural for the retaining wall at their sports field. Most recently I was hired as a consultant to help create a mosaic entryway at the Portville Central School.

These public art projects are so special to me because I get a chance to share some of what I know about working with clay. I feel that it is important to have public art for the community to experience.

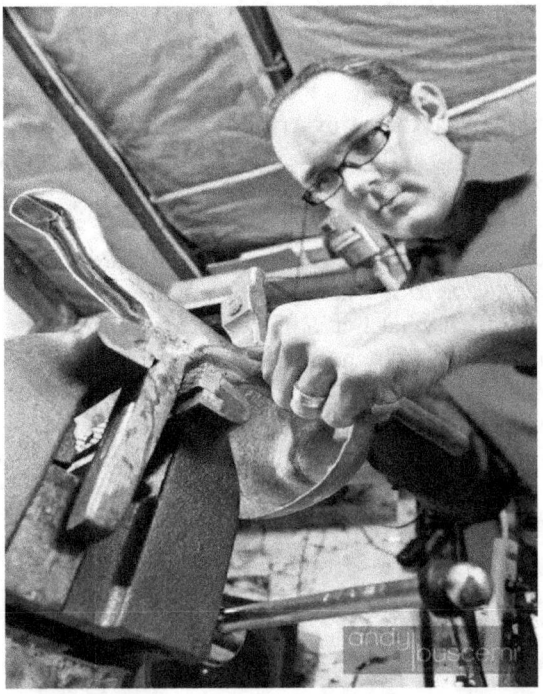

Describe your artistic specialty and what you typically like to create.

I create handmade metal art objects and jewelry in copper, silver, bronze and gold. My specialty techniques include chasing, repoussé and hand engraving.

My work has been going in the direction of hand engraving so I've been working smaller. I'm one of the only gun engravers in Western New York, and I also do jewelry engraving. That's kind of the direction I'll go as my hands get more and more stressed from rigorous metal work.

Who/what are your inspirations, and why?

I have been inspired by Japanese work and the mission style. I minored in woodworking at RIT and my woodwork was very mission style with a lot of linear elements. My metalwork was more Japanese inspired — which of course during the Arts and Crafts period they were also looking at the Japanese aesthetic, mixing it with a medieval kind of look. If you look at the Roycroft Campus, it looks medieval.

That brings me to one of my jobs when I was in high school and I worked for a Renaissance fair. That's what brought me into metal, really, because I wanted to make armor.

I also use a lot of nature themes for inspiration. There are certain plants that I like better than others, such as the ginkgo tree which is, of course, a Japanese tree. The Korean dogwood is the one that they have over at the Roycroft Inn and I like that flower as well, which is a four-petal flower. And of course the trilliums.

I also like art nouveau and sometimes I'll branch into doing some things like that.

Describe the space where you typically create, and what is so special about that place?

I have two studio spaces in which I work. One is a home studio for smaller jobs like jewelry engraving, and a larger shop for more involved projects.

Where can people see and/or purchase your art?

My sales are only through a limited amount of shows including the Roycroft festivals and the Grove Park Inn Arts and Crafts Conference. Locally I sell from the Copper Shop Gallery on the Roycroft Campus, a logical place to look for copper work in the Roycroft tradition.

When someone looks at something you have created, what type of reaction or emotion do you hope to see, and why?

It is my hope that what I create becomes a treasured family heirloom. I do want the objects that I make to be used, but also cherished.

The art that I really strive to make are the one-of-a-kind and high-end pieces. I put enough energy and design into them that I don't want to see my pieces going up for sale on eBay. I want people who purchase my work to hold onto those pieces and pass them on from generation to generation.

Photo by Andy Buscemi Photography

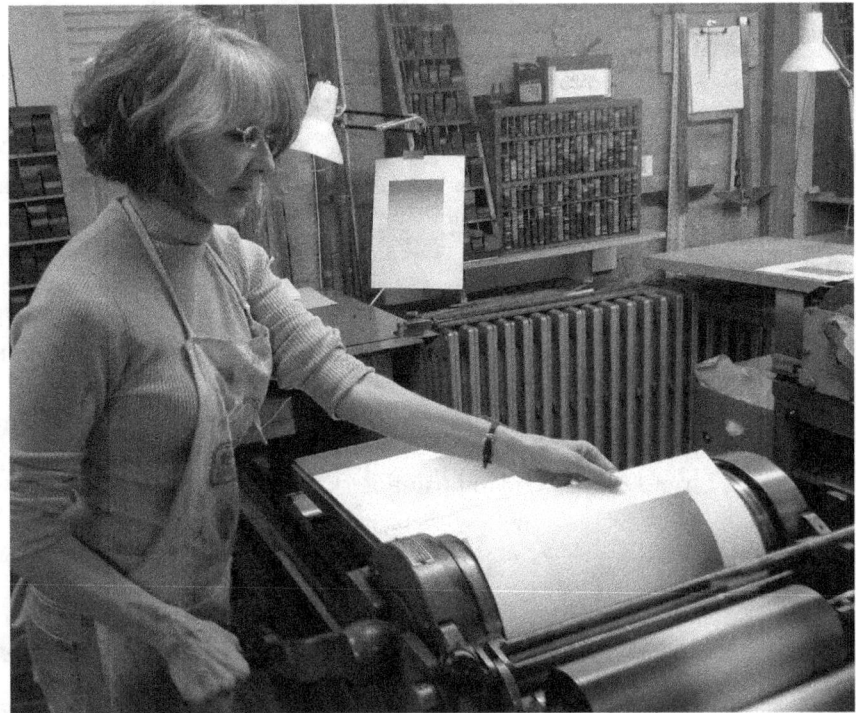

Describe your artistic specialty and what you typically like to create.

I am a Roycroft Renaissance Master Artisan in printmaking, specializing in block printing. Despite that label, I will probably never feel I've truly mastered this medium. Block printing is technically really difficult, whether you're using the spoon method or letterpress, multiple block or reduction. I'm 20 years in and still finding new ways to screw up. But I love the strong graphic quality of the block print. If done well, the picture reads from across the room.

My current favorite subject seems to be light filtering through trees, and the beautiful spaces that it creates. It's a fun challenge to take a photo of a clearing in the woods, for instance, and simplify it down to just a few colors and details in order to make the block print, while keeping the original sense of light and magic. Even after "cartoonizing" it, it has to still feel like a real place to the viewer and evoke that same sense of enchantment I felt there.

I have also been a Roycroft Renaissance Artisan in painting for several years. Painting is my refuge when I need a break from the rigors of printmaking, whether it's oil landscapes on canvas or block print-style paintings in gouache. I hope to spend more time at the easel and further develop my own voice, taking full advantage of the soft, glowy, blending capabilities of oils.

Who/what are your inspirations, and why?

Stylistically, my inspiration comes mostly from a bunch of dead guys.

William Nicholson's character block prints were a revelation to me. He did an entire alphabet of really interesting English characters: "The Milkmaid," "The

Quaker," "The Executioner." They were bold, simple, black-and-white with hand-applied watercolor tints. They said to me, "This is the perfect medium for your 'Artisans at Work' idea! Go learn it!"

Later I discovered Gustave Baumann's prints of the Southwest, with their gorgeous color palettes, and was moved to try landscapes. I've been told my "Grandma's Road I" and "Brookfield Pond" seem Baumann-esque, which is a huge compliment.

I fell in love with the flat, flowing patterns of William Morris, C.F.A. Voysey and Will Bradley. You can see their influence in my "Peace Motto," "Woman On Couch" and "The Quilter." I created spiral patterns in metallic gold a la Gustave Klimt in "The Quilter II."

The brilliant poster artist Ludwig Hohlwein also used flattened patterns and played around with positive and negative space, which I experimented with in "Lady Golfer" and "Woman On Couch," where a shaded part of a person becomes the background of the picture.

Maxfield Parrish's brilliant cobalt skies have shown up in "The Gloaming" and "High Desert Juniper."

And as I try to sharpen my oil painting skills, I will plaster the studio with printouts of paintings by Sargent and Anders Zorn. I'm in awe of their ability to paint a person who seems so alive and real, while using big, juicy, seemingly casual swooshes of the brush!

Do you travel from show to show? What are the best and worst aspects of life on the road? Feel free to share your most memorable story.

I average 15 to 20 shows per year, many of which are outdoor art festivals. Up until about six years ago, I did them alone. Now I am totally spoiled because my husband has become my business partner and carries much of the load, figuratively and literally. Now I wouldn't dream of trying to do it without Road Crew Bob.

I have ever-changing feelings about shows. Shows are both thrilling and exhausting. They connect us with my audience but leave us depleted. They steal my art-making time but provide us with much of our income. We vacillate between saying, "Need more art-making time, must do fewer shows!" and "Hey, let's try to get into this show, I hear it's really good!"

The best thing for me, after months of creating and wondering if it's any good, is to watch people walk into the booth and fall in love with the work. My mission is to make pictures that uplift people, so it's hugely satisfying to see the pictures do their job.

The worst thing is dealing with bad weather. The second worst thing is having a difficult set-up. There was one show we used to do where we always had both. The setup that usually takes us about eight hours had to be done in three hours, and our booth had a curb running through it, so the back of the tents and walls were eight inches higher than the front. Road Crew Bob fashioned a clever system that put the front of the booth up on blocks to even it out.

The show began, we were already frazzled, and prices still hadn't been put on the art. Along came a thunderstorm, followed by a flash flood flowing right through our booth along the curb. I went to see how the artist in the booth next to me was managing, and as I stood there I saw several things from my booth floating downstream through her booth! We lost about 50 posters, and many matted block prints got damp. That night our hotel room was covered with drying prints.

Where can people see and/or purchase your art?

Years ago I launched a website, www.laurawilder.com, and Webmaster Bob keeps upgrading and improving it. Now it is a very user-friendly online store, as well as a good source of information about upcoming events, retail shops that carry my work, block printing, my background and my blog. It also invites folks to sign up for my e-newsletter, which I send out about once a month.

It seems like people are doing more online shopping than ever (I know I am), so I am grateful that there's an easy way for people to see and purchase my work from home. Customer Service Agent Bob takes care of any special requests, and Shipping Clerk Bob is packing and shipping things almost on a daily basis.

Besides all the Bobs, I am grateful to my framing people: Thomas Pafk and Howard Lehning, both Roycroft Renaissance Master Artisans who make exquisite frames, and Cindy Bailey, who cuts all of our mats and assembles the art in the frames. The quarter-sawn oak frames get almost as much attention as the art does!

As an artist, what is the best piece of advice that you were ever given? What words of inspiration or advice would you offer those who might aspire to follow in your artistic footsteps?

The best art advice I ever got came from my very non-artsy husband, during our (very brief) courtship. While I was in Chicago setting up for a show, a dozen red roses were delivered to my booth, along with a little book called Follow Your Bliss. This little book was all about not being afraid to take risks, to believe in yourself, and to pursue your passions.

It was a significant moment for me for a few reasons. First, like most artists, I had received my share of well-meaning warnings that I could never make a living as an artist, and perhaps I should get a real job and let art be my hobby. I often wondered if they were right, and at times it slowed my progress. But here was this great guy cheering me on.

Secondly, I had had recurring bouts of artistic self-doubt throughout my career. In college, my style was out of sync with current trends in fine art. As a commercial artist, my style wasn't quite commercial enough. Even as a Roycroft Renaissance Artisan, I often struggled with artist's block or took on commissioned projects that didn't really interest me artistically, thinking I had to shelve my own ideas in order to make a living.

Since that day in Chicago I've tried to stay truer to my visions, and I think it shows in the work and in the wonderful response I get from my collectors.

So I give aspiring artists, or anybody really, the same advice: The thing you are good at and passionate about is the gift you are meant to share with the world. Learn about how to make a successful business with it and go do it. And find a mate who will cheer you on!

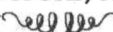

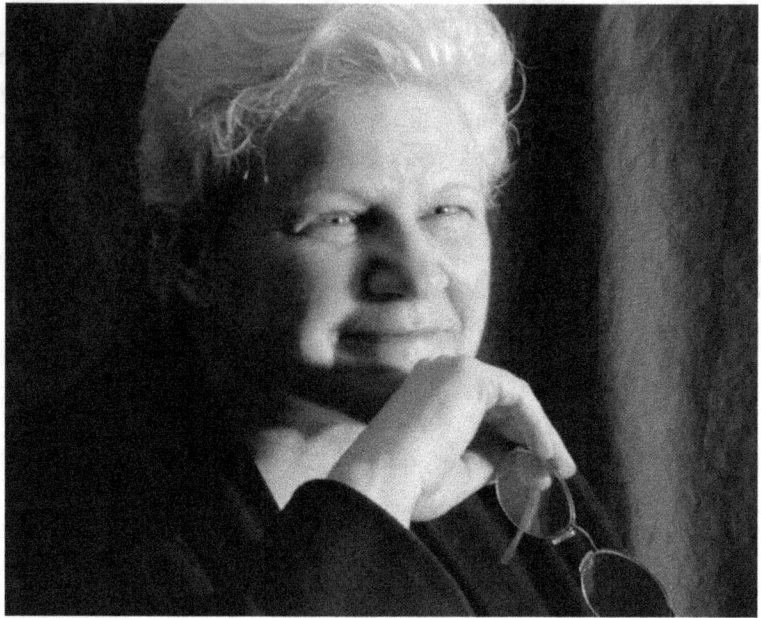

Describe your artistic specialty and what you typically like to create.

My specialty is in creating and glazing large cone 10-fired ceramic stoneware tiles. I also design and fabricate the oak frame for each. For me the frame is important and I consider it part of the overall artistic intent. I especially like to create a tile and frame that, when combined, tell a story.

Describe the space where you typically create, and what is so special about that place?

I love working in my studio which consists of a large room with a partial cathedral ceiling. The area also has northern light on one side. Over the years I have worked hard to acquire equipment — tables, storage cabinets, etc. — that were made from around 1900 to 1925. For example, there are two drafting/work tables with cast iron legs as well as a mahogany dental cabinet and a Hamilton oak typeset cabinet which function as storage units to house many of my tools and supplies. My studio also has a door wall in which I created two large glass windows from a Tiffany-style landscape so as to add colorful ambiance to my workspace. I like to feel as though I have the most technologically advanced "19th century" art studio around!

Where can people see and/or purchase your art?

My framed art tiles can be seen annually at the Arts and Crafts Conference held at the Grove Park Inn in Asheville, North Carolina. Because it is always better to see the artwork in person, my framed art tiles are also regularly available at the Roycroft Gallery as well as at the gallery at Pewabic Pottery, Detroit, Michigan. An example of the type of frame art tiles I create can also be seen via my website at www.witkowskiartworks.com.

As an artist, what is the best piece of advice that you were ever given? What words of inspiration or advice would you offer those who might aspire to follow in your artistic footsteps?

The best advice ever given to me as an artist was, "There are three things that are important in becoming a successful/satisfied artist. First, you need the talent. Second, you need a good instructor. And third and most important, because without it the other two are useless ... you need discipline!"

When someone looks at something you have created, what type of reaction or emotion do you hope to see, and why?

I want my framed art tiles to take the viewer someplace special and specific to them! That experience was typified beautifully a few years ago from a young man who, with his two-year-old son in a stroller, was viewing one of my framed art tiles depicting a nighttime scene of a rook against a large moon. The glint in his eye said it all but then he turned to me and said, "You know, when I look at this tile I can hear the crickets chirping!"

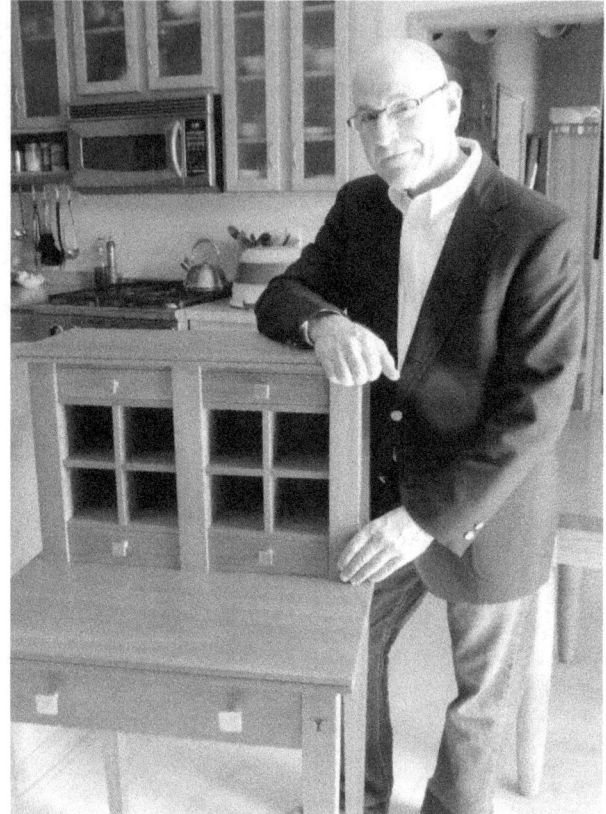

Describe your artistic specialty and what you typically like to create.

My artistic endeavors typically reside in the wood studio, specifically furniture. As I look back at four decades of furniture making, tables seem to be the form I chose most to interpret. I have often speculated why but cannot point to a particular reason or event to solve the mystery; the vast majority of ideas just materialize that way.

It has often been said that the historical evolution of furniture design is very incestuous, and as I look back on my designs I am compelled to agree. My parents were avid collectors of artifacts and my exposure to those wonderful historic pieces clearly influenced my designs.

Conceptual cultivation is essential for any design and those that are rushed into production are doomed even before selection of the raw materials. Ideas take critical thought to evolve and one must learn to be patient and nurture the process.

What is your attraction to the Roycroft arts community and the Roycrofters-At-Large Association? How has it impacted you as an artist?

The Roycroft Artisans are a unique collection of extremely talented designers and craftspeople. The combined historical knowledge of the fields, the technical abilities and artistic sensibilities in this group are astounding. It is a humbling experience to be associated with them and I know they have pushed me to be more proficient in every aspect of my craft. I am honored to be a member of this association.

As an artist, what is the best piece of advice that you were ever given? What words of inspiration or advice would you offer those who might aspire to follow in your artistic footsteps?

Being a craftsperson is a calling, and the louder the voice the greater the chances of success. Listen to the voice and then throw yourself, with reckless abandon, heart and soul, into the technical training, knowledge of historical styles, awareness of the creative world around you (regardless of medium), familiarity with the current leaders of your field and an ever-evolving sense of design and creative expression.

Then save every shekel you can to purchase the finest tools of your trade and apprentice yourself to a kind and generous master (and stay longer than you think you need to). Once there, keep your eyes and ears open and your mouth shut. Only speak to ask questions that are well thought out; ones that you have genuinely challenged yourself to answer first. Learn to brainstorm every possible technical and aesthetic scenario that you observe in the studio. This will help train you for when you are alone in your own studio.

If you follow these simple rules and have an unwavering passion for your field, are not afraid of hard work and dedication, embrace constructive criticism, can learn from your failures and you pray to the design gods every night, you have a better than average chance of success.

When someone looks at something you have created, what type of reaction or emotion do you hope to see, and why?

Every designer/craftsperson wants recognition for what we have labored over for countless hours. Accolades from ignorance are fine but it does not satiate the need for feedback from individuals who understand the sacrifice, recognize and appreciate technical virtuosity and possess an elevated sense of design. These people are intimately familiar with the craft and are sympathetic to the lifestyle. Ultimately, reactions from those people are what I am striving for and comments from the informed are additional motivators that drive me to create.

I have never met an artist, designer or craftsperson who didn't have an ego, some greater than others. However, a normal ego is essential and preferred.

Do you have an artistic goal — a bucket list project — that hasn't yet been met?

As a young apprentice I saw a picture of this small oak writing table in a book I was reading. It was a well-designed gem with beautiful but simple lines, wonderful symmetry and interesting details. The book was full of amazing images and I eventually turned the page to see more. Unfortunately, I didn't record any pertinent facts about the piece, the designer or the book, and it was gone.

Many years later, when I was developing a course involving the history of furniture design, I found it again. The piece had the same profound effect upon me as when I first witnessed it years before. This time I documented the details. The table was attributed to the English Arts and Crafts designer Arthur Heygate Mackmurdo back in 1886. I made photocopies and pinned them to a wall in my studio.

We conversed for many years until I finally summoned the will to pick up my favorite pencil and start drawing. The conversation continued sporadically for another few years; what to incorporate and what not. The danger for any designer who wants to develop their own voice is to borrow too much. It's about capturing its essence and paying homage to its creator. Something that inspires must only become a point of departure and your voice creates the piece that inspires the next generation.

I am very pleased with my interpretation of Master Mackmurdo's desk and hope he is too. I truly feel that this particular piece summarizes my career as a designer and craftsman.

ADDITIONAL ROYCROFT RENAISSANCE MASTER ARTISANS

Dayna Banka-Slone, *Master, Metal Jewelry*

Ellen Chandler, *Master, Leather*

Eileen DelDuca, *Master, Jewelry*

Howard Lehning, *Master, Wood*

Natalie Richards, *Master, Hand Embroidery*

IN MEMORIAM: KITTY TURGEON, FOUNDER AND CHAMPION OF THE ARTISANS

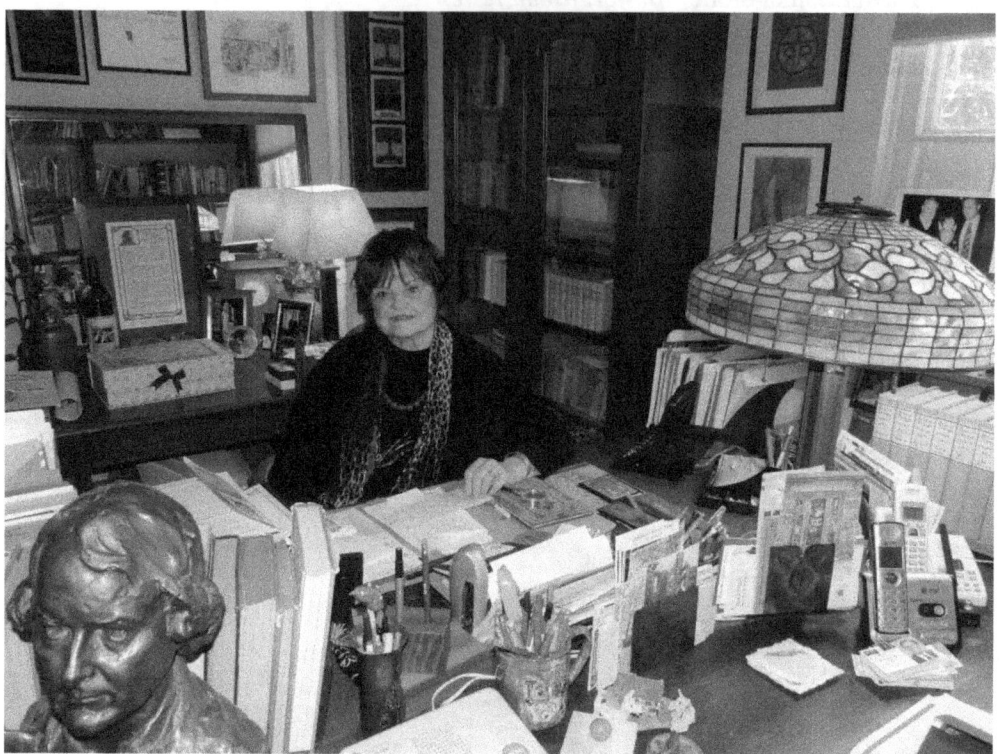

(I wrote this profile in January 2014 following an inspiring interview with Kitty Turgeon, one of the original founders of the Roycrofters-At-Large Association. Kitty passed away on Nov. 3, 2014. — Joe Kirchmyer)

Years ago, if you wanted to learn about a particular subject, you would head off to your local library to find books related to the topic or page through Encyclopedia Britannica. As computers made their way into practically every home and classroom, the information was literally at our fingertips, a mouse click away if you will.

If you want information without delay, search engines like Google and the online encyclopedia Wikipedia are invaluable tools. In fact, if you "google" the word "Roycroft," you'll find approximately 1.35 million results! And no, that's not a typo.

But there's another way to learn about a subject. It's called conversation, and it puts the heart and soul into the exchange of information.

On Friday, January 10, I had the privilege of sitting down for a 90-minute "interview" with Edythe "Kitty" Turgeon, one of the four founding members — along with Nancy Hubbard Brady, Charles Hamilton and Rixford Jennings — of the Roycrofters-At-Large Association. At 80 years of age, today she is the only living member of that small but impressive think tank.

I went into our meeting with a list of eight questions written in my notebook. After being welcomed into her Walnut Street home — the Fournier House on the

National Historic Landmark Roycroft Campus in East Aurora — she invited me to sit in one of her Roycroft chairs which she called "the most comfortable seat in the house." While engaging in light conversation, I sat in awe of the Arts and Crafts "museum" that surrounded me. Eventually, I turned on my tape recorder and asked my first question: "Limiting yourself to just a couple of sentences, tell me about Kitty Turgeon."

I'm not sure if I actually asked another question.

For 90 minutes, Kitty took me on an incredible Roycroft adventure, sharing her insider information about the Roycroft Campus, the Roycrofters-At-Large Association, the philosophy of Elbert Hubbard and her entry into the Roycroft way of life. As a Roycroft novice, I'm not ashamed to admit that 90 percent of the information went way over my head. But I was completely captivated. Ninety minutes flew by in the blink of an eye.

So who is Kitty Turgeon?

"I am, by profession, an interior designer," she said. "That's the fancy title."

Over the course of our conversation, I would also learn that she holds a master's degree from the School of Hotel Administration at Cornell University, is part of the famous Turgeon family of restauranteurs, and is a published author. In fact, I was honored to leave our meeting with a signed copy of "Images of America, The Roycroft Campus," in my hands.

But most of all I learned that Kitty Turgeon is a living encyclopedia filled with Roycroft knowledge, every vivid memory another page of the incredible history book that resides inside her head and heart. (Actually, Kitty is in the process of writing another Roycroft book, which I'll explain later.)

As I put pen to paper during our conversation, I placed a star next to my notes when Kitty said something that, for whatever reason, I found to be quite fascinating. And rather than go back and try to make sense of the mind-blowing information that was shared — a task that might take me weeks, months, years to fully understand — I thought I would share with you some of my favorite quotes from that encounter and encourage you to sit down with Kitty, or any of the talented Roycroft Artisans, to learn as much as you possibly can about them and their dedication to their craft.

Here are some of those memorable moments ...

• "The Roycrofters-At-Large name was Charlie's contribution, the mark was Rix's and Nancy coined the term 'Roycroft Renaissance.' I was the one who owned the buildings and was the 'youngster' who could run around and sort of make things happen."

• "The Roycrofters-At-Large Association didn't put East Aurora on the map. The horses in Hamlim Park put it on the map, but Hubbard came here because of the horses, because his parents started their married life on the Seneca Reservation and because he knew the reputation of this particular area being Native American holy ground. I think it's one of the magic qualities or components of Roycroft that makes it such a centerpiece because it's like a magnet. Artistic, musical, theatre, crafts, art — they're all somehow magnetized to the place! And I certainly felt that magnetism the minute I walk in the door."

• "My job (as innkeeper of the Roycroft Inn) was to make it look like it was supposed to look. But it was ghastly! We spent hundreds of thousands of dollars on the place over the years, redecorating it really to make it look more authentic. It became pretty obvious within the first five years that it needed millions. Hundreds of thousand weren't going to do it. I imagine when they're through, this will be going on a $25 to $50 million dollar project to restore the campus, just like the Martin Complex."

• "I realized we needed to get the Roycroft up to National Landmark status. In October 1985, the Republicans were having a fundraiser here for Congressman Jack Kemp. I went up to him and said 'Well, Jack, is everything OK with the food and drinks ... and will you help me cut the cake? He later asked me, 'What can I do to help?' I asked if he could help move our landmark status along, and he said he would see what he could do. (The process actually began back in 1976.) By November we were in Washington where they were having a meeting for potential landmark applicants. They then read off an alphabetical list of nine candidates who would get the designation that year. The list started with Alcatraz and ended with Roycroft."

• Most Roycrofters-At-Large Association members don't know that it is through our organization that we achieved National Landmark status. We're 38 years old now and of the current board of directors, only a few of us go all the way back. Other than Al Sleeper, Howard Lehning and I, nobody really remembers the beginning and all of the things that we accomplished."

• "Al was president when the sculpture went up on Main Street. The steel was donated for it — it's reject torpedo steel, which is exactly how Alice and Elbert (Hubbard) died." While passengers aboard the RMS Lusitania in 1915, the ship was torpedoed and sunk by a German u-boat.

• "The Roycroft has a life of its own. You cannot be as closely connected 24/7 to it as I have all of these years and not know that this place has a life of its own."

• "It isn't the handcrafted 'stuff' that interests me so much as the (Roycroft) spirituality and philosophy. That is the part that turns me on because it's so profound. I've read a lot of Elbert Hubbard. I've read Alice Hubbard. It was their daughter Miriam who told me if you want to know about the Roycroft, read Elbert Hubbard because it's the only way you'll really get a feel for what they wanted to do."

• "All these years ... I feel like I've been guided — as if I was under sealed orders or something, and I didn't know what was steering the direction. Except, I just knew what I was supposed to do. Now that I've been a member of the Rosicrucians for the past 10 years, I know where that comes from." (Elbert and Alice Hubbard were members of the Rosicrucian Order.)

• "I'd like to think that my role is not just focusing on Roycroft but the interconnection of of the whole Arts and Crafts movement. Arts and Crafts is not a style, it's a way of life. It's a big umbrella of a philosophy. It's all different styles based on one thing. It's all about nature. It's all about saving our planet."

Kitty plans to share more of her knowledge in a new book — two or three volumes are planned — on the renaissance of the Roycroft, "from 1960 to whenever ... as long as I live and keep going," she said with a hearty laugh. "That's my big ambition right now, to finish the book. Two hip replacements got in the way the last couple of years!"

And if you purchase a copy, ask Kitty to sign the book for you as you might expect to find the following inscription: "Hand, Head & Heart! Best & Blessings, Kitty Turgeon." It's what I was so happy to discover when I opened "Images of America, The Roycroft Campus," for the very first time.

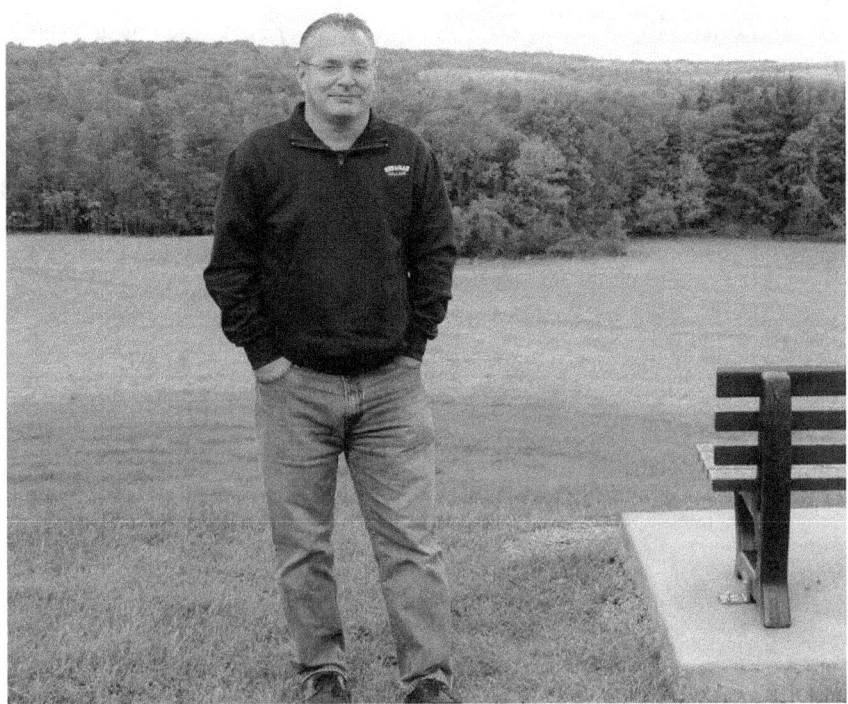

Joe Kirchmyer has enjoyed writing and storytelling since an early age. He earned a bachelor's degree in journalism from Buffalo State College and after graduation went to work for several weekly newspapers in the Western New York area. After a nearly three-year stint in corporate marketing, he joined *The Buffalo News* where he worked for twenty years and oversaw the production of advertisements and special sections too numerous to count.

In 2009 he fulfilled a lifelong dream and opened his own small business, a communications company called Kirchmyer Media LLC. The company, based in Joe's hometown of West Seneca, New York, not far from the Roycroft Campus, caters to the communication needs of nonprofit organizations and other small businesses throughout Western New York and Southern Ontario. He is especially proud of the marketing work he does for the Roycrofters-At-Large Association.

In 2011, Joe's first book, "Diamonds in the Rough," was published by No Frills Buffalo. (Special thanks to Mark Pogodzinski, founder of No Frills Buffalo, for all of his hard work and incredible support!) Diamonds in the Rough is a compilation of short stories with sports and inspirational themes. His second book, "Most Likely to Survive," also published by No Frills Buffalo, details the incredible story of Matthew Faulkner, a young man who overcame long odds to recover from a significant traumatic brain injury. Joe has also provided photography and editing services for a number of other books, publications and websites.

In addition to writing, Joe enjoys photography, dogs, the great outdoors and just about every sport ever played, especially softball. He's also known to be a collector of sports memorabilia, art and historical items. With a business partner, Jeff Surdej of

Surdej Web Solutions, he recently launched a popular new website, BuffaloScoop.com.

Joe is married to his wife of 30 years, Maureen, and together they have two children, Andrew and Lauren.

To contact Joe or to schedule an interview or speaking engagement, please send an email to jkirchmyer@verizon.net.